LIVING
NATIONS,
LIVING
WORDS

LIVING
NATIONS,
LIVING
WORDS

AN ANTHOLOGY OF FIRST PEOPLES POETRY

COLLECTED AND WITH AN INTRODUCTION BY
JOY HARJO, 23RD U.S. POET LAUREATE

FOREWORD BY CARLA D. HAYDEN, LIBRARIAN OF CONGRESS

W. W. NORTON & COMPANY
Independent Publishers Since 1923

For information about special discounts for bulk purchases, please contact
W. W. Norton Special Sales at specialsales@wwnorton.com or 800-233-4830

Manufacturing by LSC Communications Harrisonburg
Book design by Chris Welch
Production manager: Julia Druskin

Library of Congress Cataloging-in-Publication Data

Names: Harjo, Joy, editor. | Hayden, Carla Diane, 1952– writer of foreword. |
Library of Congress, issuing body.
Title: Living nations, living words : an anthology of first peoples poetry / collected
and with an introduction by Joy Harjo, 23rd U.S. Poet Laureate ; foreword by
Carla D. Hayden, Librarian of Congress.
Description: First edition. |
New York : W. W. Norton & Company, [2021] | Includes index.
Identifiers: LCCN 2021005778 | ISBN 9780393867916 (paperback) |
ISBN 9780393867923 (epub)
Subjects: LCSH: American poetry—Indian authors. | American poetry—
21st century. | Indians of North America—Poetry.
Classification: LCC PS591.I55 L56 2021 | DDC 811.008/0897—dc23
LC record available at https://lccn.loc.gov/2021005778

W. W. Norton & Company, Inc., 500 Fifth Avenue, New York, N.Y. 10110
www.wwnorton.com

W. W. Norton & Company Ltd., 15 Carlisle Street, London W1D 3BS

1 2 3 4 5 6 7 8 9 0

Contents

BECOMING/EAST

CENTER/NORTH–SOUTH

DEPARTURE/WEST

Foreword

During her inaugural reading as the twenty-third Poet Laureate Consultant in Poetry to the Library of Congress, Joy Harjo said, "Every poem has poetry ancestors." The poet laureateship has had a long line of esteemed ancestors over its eighty-plus-year history. Since 1937, the Library of Congress has appointed such luminaries as Elizabeth Bishop, Robert Frost, Gwendolyn Brooks, and Robert Pinsky. As Joy Harjo performed that evening in the Library's Coolidge Auditorium—reciting her poems, playing the flute and saxophone, and rocking out to her backing musicians—it was easy to imagine that the spirits of these past laureates were cheering her on, alongside the overflow audience who gave her a standing ovation.

The electricity in the air that night is a typical response to Harjo—a poet, author, musician, playwright, mentor, and advocate for social justice. As the first Native poet to serve as poet laureate, Harjo (a member of the Muscogee [Creek] Nation) has focused on showing that Native people and poets are alive and thriving, and have vital and unequivocal roots in this country. This anthology is one manifestation of her signature laureate project, which includes an online map of contemporary Native poets. By clicking on the map, users can immerse themselves in these poets' worlds: see where each poet lives or feels most rooted, read their poems and biographies, and—best of all—hear their voices and languages as they recite and discuss their poems. This remarkable body of work, titled "Living Nations, Living Words," forms the foundation of a new online collection in the Library's American Folklife Center, and is reprinted here as a physical companion to Joy's digital project.

As Joy said, "Poetry doesn't just emerge, it emerges from the soul of a community." There are so many communities to discover and explore at the Library of Congress. I invite you to visit loc.gov to experience Joy's "Living Nations, Living Words" project, along with other inspiring literary resources and collections such as Poetry 180, Poetry of America, and the Archive of Recorded Poetry and Literature.

—Carla D. Hayden, Librarian of Congress

Introduction

The very first maps were drawn into the earth with stick or stone implements. They told us where we lived, the location of food, water, and danger. Some were star maps of the heavens, histories notched and painted, or symbols of stories that gave directions on how to live. The earliest indigenous maps of North America were not drawn. The placement and orientation of a village, its buildings, and even mound structures were markers that mirrored the meaning of the heavens, or other directional senses. Even a basket could be a map, or a song. We carry maps of destiny in our poems.

One of the earliest existing maps, known as *Imago Mundi*, is a cuneiform tablet of the Babylonian world estimated to be from the sixth century BCE. The map shows Babylon on the Euphrates River surrounded by other nations. What I appreciate most is the language of the text that accompanies the map. One region is described as "the winged bird ends not his flight"; another is "the light is brighter than that of sunset or stars," or "where a horned bull lives and attacks the newcomer."

When I started my term as the twenty-third U.S. poet laureate I immediately began considering a signature project. As the first Native Nations poet laureate, I was aware that indigenous peoples of our country are often invisible or are not seen as human. Or we are known from false images and narratives carried over from the vitriol of New England Puritan Cotton Mather and others who imagined us as demonic heathens not capable of civilized and ordered thought and action. You will rarely find us in the cultural storytelling of America, and we are nearly nonexistent in the American book of poetry. For my project, I conceived the idea of mapping the United States based on the poetry of Native Nations poets. I liked the idea of mapping America by poetry with poets.

This anthology includes the poets and poems featured in the online mapping project. These are representative poets from locations across the country. Each poet chose their poem based on the theme of place and displacement, and with four touchpoints in mind: visibility, persistence, resistance, and acknowledgment. They also chose where they wished to place themselves—where they currently live, in their homelands, or where they feel most rooted. In the digital project, you can see the map and the poets' locations, read their poems, and hear them recite and comment on their poems.

Native roots run deep, even when people are relocated, as were many Native Nations in this country. One of the best-known relocation projects is the Trail of Tears, which removed the Cherokee, Muscogee (Creek), Seminole, Choctaw, and Chickasaw from homelands in the Southeast to Indian Territory, which is present-day Oklahoma. Like those in other communities, we travel far from home for work, opportunity, or love.

You will find some of the poets living far from their homelands. Jennifer Foerster lives in San Francisco, California. She claims this city by the ocean as her home. Her mother's family is from the prominent Perryman family of the Muscogee (Creek) Nation who lived outside of Tulsa. Her family roots go back to Georgia and Alabama. And there are poets who stay close to home, like Henry Real Bird of the Crow Nation, who grew up on his reservation speaking his native language. He started out as a bronc rider, but an injury during his college years began his journey from the demanding physicality of bronc riding to what he has called the "spiritual world" of writing.

There were also other considerations when making the map. When editing or curating any Native Nation project the question always arises: who is indigenous? We have chosen to allow tribal nations to define who is a tribal member. It is not up to us to be the arbitrators.

There are many other Native Nations poets—from more than 573 federally recognized Native Nations and other legitimate state-recognized tribal entities—who deserve to be included. Many of us are established in our communities, known in languages other than English. There are those coming up who are the purl of the next wave of young indigenous poets. We are like any other living American poets who venture into the craft with the tools of knowledge and creativity to ride the waves of language, even as we also tend to our indigenous cultural systems and communities. Our common language of English, or sometimes Spanish, is a crossing place, as is poetry a common language and crossing place to meet many from all over the world.

These Native Nations poets and their poems included in this anthology therefore become representative of a much deeper and wider field of poetry.

The poems here are not organized around geography. We could begin anywhere on the map, for each place might be the navel place of a creation story, somewhere in the middle of the story, or a place of departure. We begin with the East, or Becoming. The Eastern Seaboard and bordering states were the site of the major push of colonization. The tribal nations here were inspirational to the root culture of America. The Iroquois and Muscogee (Creek) peoples inspired the American democratic government even as these Native Nations were diminished by history. East is considered the direction of becoming, the sunrise place.

Some of the poems in this section fit symbolically rather than geographically, like "Daybreak" by Jake Skeets, the poem that opens the Becoming/East section. This poem literally provides the template for the anthology's shape, each section marking the place as the sun of knowing moves from dawn to evening. Each of these poems establishes that heritage is a living thing, and there can be no heritage without land and the relationships that outline our kinship.

In the Center, or North–South, we are at the middle of the country, far away from the Atlantic or the Pacific Oceans, in that physical place which metaphorically represents the belly and the heart of presence and knowledge, of understanding. It is the place of crossroads. These are poems of affirmation, humor, and fury. When reading these poems, you will retreat to tears, to silence created by grief or joy, or laugh aloud. Mahealani Perez-Wendt's poem is placed here because it centers itself at a crossroads of struggle. "Na Wai Eā, The Freed Waters" is a genealogy of a struggle to uphold the relationship between the taro and human relatives, the struggle for rightful use of water, and for the rights of water to be returned home.

As with any map, we are invested in where we are going. This brings us to the last section: Departure, or West. Here we are looking forward, into the future, constructing fresh meaning from knowledge passed to us by our ancestors and weaving it with fresh experience. The design emerges in our poetry as words, images, and other poetic elements combine with unknown forces.

Navajo poet Luci Tapahonso's "Ilíigo Naalyéhé: Goods of Value" deconstructs the Navajo way of being and understanding the world: how soft goods of value are those ideals of knowing and behavior, and how they appear in mythical and philosophical constructs. These soft goods find their way into the constructions of what we use, or hard goods such as weavings, baskets, and jewelry, even poetry.

To conclude the mapping is "Postcolonial Love Poem" by Natalie Diaz. The lover and beloved in the poem are the earth, located by lyric in liminal eternity. Yet both are bound by a postcolonial map that would divide, even destroy, them. Before colonization we knew ourselves as earth without question. As we love, we come to know who we truly are, as nations, families, as lovers: "Until then, we touch our bodies like wounds— / The war never ended and somehow begins again."

Now, we have a map. The soft goods are the mapmaking materials. The mapmaking represented by this anthology comes at a crucial time in history, a time in which the failures to acknowledge, listen to, and consider everyone when making the map of American memory has brought us to a reckoning.

I appreciate how Sherwin Bitsui expresses the quandary of being an indigenous poet writing in English with a Navajo mind and sense of language. As he says in his online commentary for this project, "These two systems merge to create a world attempting to restore itself when change is inevitable."

Maybe we are at the place where many roads come together under the dimming sun. We must make a new map, together where poetry is sung.
—Joy Harjo, 23rd U.S. Poet Laureate

BECOMING/EAST

JAKE SKEETS

Jake Skeets, Diné (Navajo), is Tsi'naajínii, born for Tábąąhá. He is the author of *Eyes Bottle Dark with a Mouthful of Flowers* and the winner of the 2018 National Poetry Series and the 2020 Whiting Award.

Quanah Yazzie

Daybreak

abíní hoolzish
:   the low-moon horizon turquoise serenes pink-lit
      from the pulp and fray of whorled milkweed
      summer cypress turkey-feathered struts stark pebbled
      through the sheep corral and shade house
      beneath the horse trough star thistle and nine-awned grass
      reflect night storms and rainbow through the morning
      the sun's rays darling through narrow shoots of cloud, vapor,
      or maybe morning fog

hók'ą́ą́dóó
:   above a passing plane or marsh hawk or maybe a crow
      casts its wing on the sweet yellow clover and field weed
      on the rubble of rust tin can and car axle and wheel barrow
      a basketball backboard crafted from sheet metal and piping
      the ground crickets beneath moths telling a story as butterflies
      they flail and flare through two-needle piñon and ryegrass
      cottontails squirrel into the culvert under the main road
      now wash-like, parched, its flow sands really memory for water

i'íí'ą́ k'ad

:   salsify and velvetweed overtop a broken fence

its twine, slat, and barbed wire cloaked by dusked sod

dirt road mud walls, tumbleweed, and maybe sunflowers

bow-pulled arc by the metal windmill watering faint wind

the mill echoes awake with each rock thrown

at its face, back, or the bend of its opened arms

bįįh níléíjí da'ayą́—clouds drop their shoulders into rain,

into the coral evening, into the evening's evening

OFELIA ZEPEDA

Ofelia Zepeda is the author, most recently, of *Where Clouds Are Formed*. She is Tohono O'odham and a Regents' Professor and professor of linguistics at the University of Arizona, where she is also the director of the American Indian Language Development Institute (AILDI).

Tony Celentano

B 'o E-a:g maṣ 'ab Him g Ju:kĭ

B 'o 'e-a:g maṣ 'ab him g ju:kĭ.
Ṣag wepo mo pi woho.
Nañpi koi ta:tk g jewed mat am o i si ka:ckad c pi o i-hoiñad c o
     ñenḍad.
Ṣag wepo mo pi woho.
Nañpi koi ta:tk g da:m ka:cim mat o ge s-wa'usim s-we:ckad.
Ṣag wepo mo pi woho.
Nañpi koi ta:tk g hewel mat s-hewogim o 'i-me:
Ṣag wepo mo pi woho.
Nañpi koi hewegid g s-wa'us jeweḍ
Mat g hewel 'ab o u'ad.
Nia, heg hekaj o pi ṣa'i woho matṣ o ju:.

It is Going to Rain

Someone said it is going to rain.
I think it is not so.
Because I have not felt the earth and the way it holds still
in anticipation.
I think it is not so.
Because I have not yet felt the sky become heavy with moisture of
  preparation.
I think it is not so.
Because I have not yet felt the winds move with their coolness.
I think it is not so.
Because I have not yet inhaled the sweet, wet dirt the winds bring.
So, there is no truth that it will rain.

IMAIKALANI KALAHELE

Imaikalani Kalahele, author of *Kalahele*, is a Hawaiian (Maoli) artist, poet, and philosopher. He is the son of Rebecca Keliiolalo Kalahele, from Waihee, Maui, and Dale Alton Muerlott, from Illinois; husband to Eunice; father of four; and grandfather of fifteen.

Kealiikauila Niheu

Maoli

In the beginning there was a voice
and the voice was Maoli

Singing from before
the first footprint
on our sands

This Maoli was part of the original
echo out of Po
is our ancestor

Before alii . . . before the priesthood
even before the storytellers
Maoli was heard
telling the first stories
singing the first songs
and reading the stars for the first time

Maoli . . . my brother . . . my sister . . . my father . . . my mother . . . my ancestors

Before had england
even before jesus
There was a voice
and the voice was Maoli

ELISE PASCHEN

Elise Paschen is the author of *The Nightlife, Bestiary, Infidelities,* and *Houses: Coasts.* She has edited numerous poetry anthologies and teaches in the MFA Writing Program at the School of the Art Institute of Chicago. Paschen is an enrolled member of the Osage Nation.

Jennifer Girard

Heritage

X

                      The year my mother was born

in Fairfax, Oklahoma,

                          white men were marrying Osage

            women and killing them

     for their headrights.

                    My mother was born a year after

The Indian Citizenship Act was passed—

                    Indians tied to the U.S.

        for or against their wills.

     Three years before her birth, her half sister

                Baby Ruth's grave was dynamited

with nitroglycerine by outlaws

                    scavenging for diamonds

        and gold buried inside the casket.

     In the Tallchief plot

               I wander through family history—

the marble monuments,

               angelic statues—measuring

        each step on grass,

memorizing photographs.

              This one of a striking

     beauty, my great grandmother

Eliza Bigheart Tall Chief, 1870–1962,

          surviving her husband

by fifty years. The widow, the adored

grandmother of my mother. Eliza.

Only now do I see my name

a permutation of hers.

At home in Chicago

every day I pass

family photographs framed

on walls. My great grandfather's

oval sepia portrait

of his boyish face

replicated on the headstone.

Instead of the young bride,

here is Eliza, a tribal elder,

wrapped in a multi-colored

blanket, standing outside

her front porch, a photo

taken after all those years

she outlived him.

CRAIG SANTOS PEREZ

Craig Santos Perez, a native CHamoru from the Pacific island of Guåhan (Guam), is the author of five books of poetry, including *Habitat Threshold*, and the coeditor of five anthologies. He is a professor of English at the University of Hawaiʻi at Mānoa.

Hannah Ensor

Off-Island CHamorus

My family migrated to California when I was 15 years old.
During the first day at my new high school, the homeroom
teacher asked: "Where are you from?" "The Mariana Islands,"
I answered. He replied: "I've never heard of that place.
Prove it exists." And when I stepped in front of the world map
on the wall, it transformed into a mirror: the Pacific Ocean,
like my body, was split in two and flayed to the margins. I
found Australia, then the Philippines, then Japan. I pointed
to an empty space between them and said: "I'm from this
invisible archipelago." Everyone laughed. And even though
I descend from oceanic navigators, I felt so lost, shipwrecked

on the coast of a strange continent. "Are you a citizen?"
he probed. "Yes. My island, Guam, is a U.S. territory."
We attend American schools, eat American food, listen
to American music, watch American movies and television,
play American sports, learn American history, dream
American dreams, and die in American wars. "You
speak English well," he proclaimed, "with almost no
accent." And isn't that what it means to be a diasporic
CHamoru: to feel *foreign in a domestic sense.*

Over the last 50 years, CHamorus have migrated to
escape the violent memories of war; to seek jobs, schools,
hospitals, adventure, and love; but most of all, we've migrated
for military service, deployed and stationed to bases around
the world. According to the 2010 census, 44,000 CHamorus

live in California, 15,000 in Washington, 10,000 in Texas, 7,000 in Hawaii, and 70,000 more in every other state and even Puerto Rico. We are the most "geographically dispersed" Pacific Islander population within the United States, and off-island CHamorus now outnumber our on-island kin, with generations having been born away from our ancestral homelands, including my daughters.

Some of us will be able to return home for holidays, weddings, and funerals; others won't be able to afford the expensive plane ticket to the Western Pacific. Years and even decades might pass between trips, and each visit will feel too short. We'll lose contact with family and friends, and the island will continue to change until it becomes unfamiliar to us. And isn't that, too, what it means to be a diasporic CHamoru: to feel foreign in your own homeland.

Even after 25 years away, there are still times I feel adrift, without itinerary or destination. When I wonder: What if we stayed? What if we return? When the undertow of these questions begins pulling you out to sea, remember: migration flows through our blood like the aerial roots of the banyan tree. Remember: our ancestors taught us how to carry our culture in the canoes of our bodies. Remember: our people, scattered like stars, form new constellations when we gather. Remember: home is not simply a house, village, or island; home is an archipelago of belonging.

SUZAN SHOWN HARJO

Suzan Shown Harjo (Cheyenne and Hodulgee Muscogee) is a writer, curator, and policy advocate who has helped Indigenous Peoples protect sacred places and recover more than one million acres of lands. Her poetry has been published in numerous journals and anthologies. A recipient of the Presidential Medal of Freedom and a founder of the National Museum of the American Indian, Harjo led the successful campaign against the offensive name of the Washington NFL team, and was elected in 2020 to the American Academy of Arts and Sciences.

Lucy Fowler Williams

Welcoming Home Living Beings

Today, we welcome home beloved Living Beings

       No one alive today has seen them at home, except in dreams
       No one we ever met saw them at home, except in dreams
           Yesterday, they were stolen, many generations ago
           Yesterday, they were prisoners in private houses
           Yesterday, they were locked in university basements
           Yesterday, they were poisoned and smothered in museums
           Yesterday, they were branded with numbers and price tags
           Yesterday, they were violated by prying hands and eyes
           Yesterday, they were tortured and deprived of all that nourishes
           Yesterday, they were alone, many generations ago

Today, we welcome home beloved Living Beings

       They come home to us, their many relatives
       They return after surviving a long, hard war

       They never were meant to be warriors
       They were created with holy purpose
           As teachers and doctors
           As visionaries and guides
           As children and parents
           As artists and lovers

They were created to balance our minds
       To settle the Spirits
       To solve difficult cases
       To make a peaceful way
       To make themselves beautiful

They were created by Creation and loving human hands
       As pots and baskets and boxes
       As claws and feathers and teeth
       As hides and furs and antlers
       As hooves and shells and baleen
       As pouches and bundles and gourds
       As drums and rattles and bells
       As clay and cedar and paint
       As grasses and reeds and pollen

Today, we welcome home beloved Living Beings

We, their many relatives, have known them all our lives
We, their many relatives, have missed them all our lives
       We feed their memory with sacred foods
       We nourish their memory with sacred waters
       We keep them in our circles
       We seek them in the darkest places
       We sing the songs they sing
       We dance the dances they dance
       We pray the prayers they pray
       We dream the dreams they dream

Tomorrow, after we welcome home our beloved Living Beings

    It will be as if they never left home or us, their many relatives
    It will be as if they never left home or us
    It will be as if they never left
    It will be as if they never
    It will be as if
    It will be
    It will be as if there were no yesterday
    It will be tomorrow

RAY YOUNG BEAR

Ray Young Bear, Meskwaki (Red Earth People) tribal member, is the author of *Manifestation Wolverine: The Collected Poetry of Ray Young Bear*. His bilingual poems and songs have been featured in the *New Yorker*, the *Iowa Review*, *Under a Warm Green Linden*, and *Native Voices*.

Stella Lasley-Young Bear

Wichihaka

Kemekoteweni—wewenetwi
Kemekoteweni—wewenetwi

Kemekoteweni—wewenetwi
Mekoteweni—wewenetwi
Mekoteweni—wewenetwi
Mekoteweni—wewenetwi

Netena—Wasakekwa
Netena—Wichihaka

The One I Live With

Your traditional dance dress is beautiful.
Your traditional dance dress is beautiful.

Your traditional dance dress is beautiful.
Traditional dance dress is beautiful;
Traditional dance dress is beautiful;
Traditional dance dress is beautiful.

I said to Wasakekwa.
I said to The One I Live With.

DEBORAH A. MIRANDA

Deborah A. Miranda is both an enrolled member of the Ohlone-Costanoan Esselen Nation of the Greater Monterey Bay Area and of Chumash ancestry. Her mixed-genre book *Bad Indians: A Tribal Memoir* received the 2015 PEN Oakland/Josephine Miles Literary Award. She is the Thomas H. Broadus Jr. Professor of English at Washington and Lee University in Virginia, where she teaches literature of the margins and creative writing.

Kevin Remington

Indigenous Physics: The Element Colonizatium

1. The elimination of a substance from a living organism
   follows complex chemical kinetics.
   For example, the biological half-life
   of water in a human being
   is 9 to 10 days, with adjustments
   for behavior and temperature.
   A quantity of carbon-14 will decay
   to half its original amount after 5,730 years.
   After another 5,730 years,
   one-quarter of the original will remain.
   And so on.

   Obviously, the half-life of a substance
   depends upon the substance itself—
   measure for toxicity, fierceness, sheer venom.
   The research at hand for us today, then, is clear:
   what is the half-life of Colonizatium?
   Does Colonizatium reduce to half
   its initial impact in 50 years?
   In 1000 years?
   At what point
   does Colonizatium become unstable?
   Is the half-life of Colonizatium constant over the lifetime
   of an exponentially decaying
   Indigenous body?

2. To quote a famous Indigenous physicist, *sometimes there are complications.*

The decay of a mixture of two or more materials,
which each decay exponentially but with different half-lives,
is not exponential.
Take nuclear waste.
Imagine a mixture of a rapidly decaying element *A*,
with a speedy half-life of 1 second, and more gradual decaying element *B*,
with a half-life of 1 year.
In minutes, almost all atoms of element *A* will have decayed
after repeated reductions by half, but
very few of the atoms of element *B* will have done so,
as only a small percentage of its half-life has elapsed. Thus,
the time taken for such a mixture to fall to half its original value
cannot be easily calculated.

The element Colonizatium is much like nuclear waste:
an unequal mixture of toxic events
with wildly different half-lives.
Start with invasion, war, starvation, rape, murder—
Indian boarding schools, reservations, outlawed religions,
shame.
Include an on-going bombardment of toxic events
over a period of decades:
termination, adopting-out, domestic violence, poverty,
substance addiction, incarceration rates, diabetes,
blood quantum debates, history books, mascots,

white shamanism, fake ndns, police brutality,
anger.
A periodic table of traumatic elements.

3. Given the difficulties
   in determining the half-life of Colonizatium,
   we might argue the necessity of redirecting
   our efforts into other
   more profitable calculations.
   However,
   despite the probabilistic nature of the inquiry,
   this as-yet-undiscovered formula
   is thought to be paramount for our research
   into a chronological prediction
   of the Post-Colonial state. Recent studies
   indicate that the mixing of elements in unequal toxicities
   and immeasurable psycho-social dynamics may best be gauged
   not in mathematics
   or statistics
   or theoretical constructs,

   but in the three Indigenous elements
   Story, Dance, and Song.

   In other words,
   Deep Science of a pre-Colonial origin
   such as

formulas and algorithms encoded
within ceremonial circles, drums or clappersticks,
the spiraled helix of song,
diagrams of precise footsteps
on discrete portions of empowered earth;
stories plotted like fractal geometry,
the patterned asterisms of stars,
chemical kinetics hammered out
on the bodies of rocks.

Key to such explorations—
the re-emergence
of a fourth Indigenous element:
Dreaming.
This component, long rumored to be permanently lost
or the unstable fantasy of treasure-hunters,
possesses shape-shifting abilities
which have allowed it to survive long periods of hibernation,
enabling structural recuperation and regeneration.

Preliminary work that combines Dreaming
with the three known elements
reveals two astonishing facts:

> First) a post-Colonizatium status is, in fact,
> impossible to achieve.

Second) Story, Dance, Song and Dreaming
do not calculate nor predict
the half-life of Colonizatium.

Rather,
when applied to the Colonized subject,
these four elements
hasten the decay of Colonizatium,
pull the heavy history into themselves,
break it down

the same way maize, mustard greens, pennycress,
sunflowers, Blue sheep fescue, and canola
transform heavy metals.

The same way water hyacinths suck up mercury, lead, cadmium,
zinc, cesium, strontium-90, uranium
and pesticides,

the same way bladder campion accumulates copper,
Indian mustard greens concentrate selenium, sulphur, chromium.

The same way willow, *Salix viminalis*, absorbs uranium and
petrochemicals.

And—
once the willow's bio-mass concentrates heavy metals,

once Story, Dance, Song and Dreaming do their work,
the willow rods must be woven
into baskets
in what might be called
a miraculous exponential,
were we not, of course, privy to the facts.

We must revise our aim, therefore, toward rapid
decay of Colonizatium,
or, De-Colonization.

4. Start with Story.
   Work your way
   home.

   Huwa.

ELIZABETH WOODY

Elizabeth Woody is the author of three books of poetry: *Hand into Stone*, *Luminaries of the Humble*, and *Seven Hands, Seven Hearts*. She has published essays and short fiction and is a visual artist. She is Diné (Navajo)/ Warm Springs/Wasco/Yakama and an enrolled member of the Confederated Tribes of Warm Springs Oregon.

Native Arts and Cultures Foundation

Coquille

Watching the traditional canoe

Like a sheep horn, brown and rustic, the canoe pitches to one side—takes water.
With an exterior of finality, imaginatively halved, the cedar is quite old.
Half similar or half alien is a decision.

The curl of the paddle motions on one side and its reverse.
North and southern contrasts sea faring parallels of the
equator, akin to our navel above gender, reminiscent of central connections.

A tree crest points to venerable lineage.
One must accept oscillating internal realms, the tinder of fusion,
kissing blossoms of recognition.

Light and synthesis is sustenance and growth by these terms.
What of weighted limbs of the hanged?
The orphaned children met from a momentous crux of fortune changing hands.

A vigilant helix bends into tomorrow.
Eastern rise of simple trill funnels into the high idioms of justice.
There are survivors who know ropes of ideology—the carnage.

Truly wild geese call out a black series of condolences.
Cadence of connection and rote of mutual landing
patterned to triangles gathering and deltas.

The geese travel the points between testing each moment.
Antiquity finds its anchor in turmoil. This is the forfeiture,
solace, soft compassionate wetlands in the clarity of receding drifts.

It is the rain that mixes into heap of leaves a disciplined humid scent.
Shimmer of rippling bay reaches for the bow of simple resurgence.
Brown symbolic float Affinity and certain terms of reparation.

HEATHER CAHOON

Heather Cahoon is an award-winning poet, artist, and policy scholar from the Flathead Reservation, where she is a member of the Confederated Salish and Kootenai Tribes. Her chapbook *Elk Thirst* won the Merriam-Frontier Award at the University of Montana; and her first full-length collection of poems, *Horsefly Dress*, was published in 2020.

Heather Cahoon

Baby Out of Cut-Open Woman

so-called because he was sckʷełťelénč, "cut out of the stomach"
as an infant.   Indeed, he survived the un/believable, a lucky break,
        to become the only living member of his immediate family.

Another lucky break, he won his race against the cold birds,
earning the right
to make a law that they could no longer control all the weather,
ending the age of ice.

Next, he gathered his families' bones
their marrowed limbs, each rib, forearm
and finger.
                Covering them with his blanket, he jumped over
                        four times,
bringing them,
each one
back
to life.

•

These are the stories that belong here,
that pushed up through this soil unfurling
as arrow-leaved balsamroot leaves and boulders found in unusual
places.

How else does a thing enter this world
now so changed we struggle to hear the shapes of a language
      that no longer fits every ear.
Each story word frag-
                ment   moves
over hills the highest reaches of trees
      without catching in memory.   But

the crispness of Snlaq̓éy of Kʷĺncutn like fire
crackle the flick of sound a body remembers.

(Sckʷełťelénč: "Cut out of the stomach;" the name of the part of the weather, or a weather being, whose actions brought about the end to the last Ice Age. Snlaq̓éy: Sweat lodge. Kʷĺncutn: Creator, Maker of Ways/Mannerisms, also referred to as Amotqn or Great Spirit.)

JENNIFER ELISE FOERSTER

Jennifer Elise Foerster is the author of two books of poetry, *Bright Raft in the Afterweather* and *Leaving Tulsa*. A former Wallace Stegner Fellow at Stanford, she received a 2017 NEA Creative Writing Fellowship and a Lannan Foundation Residency Fellowship. A member of the Muscogee (Creek) Nation, she lives in San Francisco.

Richard Bluecloud Castaneda

Notes from Coosa

I find you nowhere that is here or there.
Below the sunken Uchee path—iron ore.
The ridge dividing water, veined with it—
pea vine, wiregrass, short-leaf hickory.
Old fields' flood plains, indigo-dyed.
When the woods were still dense, saw palmetto,
grapes of the hills destroyed by fire
and the haw chestnut by the hatchet.
If it were easy to leave our bodies
in the fork of Red River, two mounds of earth.
If it were easy to leave you behind
in a stream clear with flowering stones—
to find you in the language where I lost you
as if you were a sentence in this poem
and this poem an archive of the forest.
But I have burned the remaining pine.
On the bluffs, strawberries thinly scattered
and in the old beaver ponds, briar root,
a bread made of it for times of famine.

LEANNE HOWE

LeAnne Howe, author of *Choctalking on Other Realities*, is a writer, playwright, poet, scholar, and filmmaker. She is the Eidson Distinguished Professor in American Literature in the Department of English at the University of Georgia and an enrolled citizen in the Choctaw Nation of Oklahoma.

Daniel McCreary

1918 Union Valley Road Oklahoma

I

Maybe it was while reading the 1918 Union Valley Bulletin
       A political handbill given John Hoggatt by a hacking cougher at the feed store
Maybe it was the sour apple gone mahogany black that he'd eaten from his wife's
    cellar stash
       He knew he should have given it to Trudy their hog
Maybe it was the six-mile walk to and from his father's farm in Stonewall
       Just to ask, need help with that heifer, Pop?
Maybe it was the burning tingling running over the top of John's head
       As if he was being roasted alive, filling him with fear

       He coughed into his fist, *no*
              Iva honey, lock the gate so the Crowder boys can't steal our cow
       He coughed into his fist, *no*
              Iva honey,
      He coughed into his fist
              Iva, so cold.

Winds like a siren whip the Junipers outside, maybe 90 per,
       He swayed left, and then right, and onto their Jenny Lind bed
          A wedding gift,
          Coveralls still on.

II

Shocked into
consciousness
by sunlight
Iva supports
herself with her
arms and leans
forward Eyes
mucus glued
Has she been
crying in
her sleep?

The bed
is cold, the
stove out Her
long black
hair matted by
high fevers. In
her dreams,
the sound
of a gurgling
brook She
looks

at John, her
teeth chattering
He is completely
blue now. She
presses on
John's
chest. Blood
and mucus slip
between his blue
lips Breathe, John,
Breathe.

Don't
worry I
gave our baby
girl to your
sister, Euda
Yesterday,
the day
before,
maybe last
week, but
she's safe.
Didn't make
a sound, just

waved bye-bye,
Bye-bye,
Mommy
bye-bye.
Like you,
she doesn't
complain Like
you, she's more
Irish than
Cherokee—
like me.

Breathe, John,
Breathe. Take
a breath, John
Hoggatt. How
many times?
Iva curls
up by his
side, played
out Who hast
never bruised
a living
flower, she
whispers. Now

I lay
me down
to sleep I
pray
the Lord
my soul to
take.
Breathe,
John.

III

The sun is yet a rumor
          Iva sleeps like the dead
Until she doesn't.
          On the third day she feels herself rising
                    Everything a moving cloud,
She observes herself in the mirror
                              Washes her mahogany cheeks
That's odd, she thinks
          Lock the gate, John,
Or the Crowder boys will steal our cow.

She coughs into her handkerchief
          John honey,

She coughs into her handkerchief
     John honey,
She coughs into her handkerchief
     Hear me.

Yes Iva
     You live in unmeaning dreams, he says,
The grave is ready.

John honey
     Stay

I washed your Sunday shirt
     Hung it on the line to dry
We can bury our faces
     In summer laundry

Taste the scent of sun
     In a field of light
          Breathing as one

     Stay

IV

Iva is dreaming again
She hears his name, John,
The sound like a bell on her tongue,
                              John
                         on
                          on
                           on
                            g-

Breathe

LAURA DA'

Laura Da' is a poet and teacher. She is Eastern Shawnee. Her first book, *Tributaries*, won the American Book Award and her newest book is *Instruments of the True Measure*, which won the Washington State Book Award in 2019.

Jarrod Da'

The Rhetorical Feminine

Gliding from the confluence of Battery Rock
to the Devil's Backbone inside the Shawnee

National Forest makes a sound I cannot
duplicate in English. With one finger tracing

the route on an atlas, my tongue wet
with nostalgia—a waterlogged migration

by touch. I seek the cities without the words.
As late somebody's 1810 there were headwater

communities of women for the express purpose of healing,
birthing, governing shared territory—crouched

in the frog-legged stance of delivery and defense.
Linguistic evidence suggests a pattern of feminization

in Shawnee rhetoric. *Nation of women,*
bellowed strangers even as river city

dialects mouthed spells that cured war like hides
and curved breech births veiled in water

to the banks of living territory. Gliding from the confluence
of Battery Rock to the Devil's Backbone

inside the Shawnee National Forest
makes a sound I cannot duplicate in English.

LEHUA M. TAITANO

Lehua M. Taitano is a queer CHamoru writer and interdisciplinary artist from Yigu, Guåhan (Guam), and cofounder of Art 25: Art in the Twenty-fifth Century. She is the author of two volumes of poetry, *Inside Me an Island* and *A Bell Made of Stones*. Taitano's work investigates modern indigeneity, decolonization, and cultural identity in the context of diaspora.

Lehua M. Taitano

Current, I

The conventional symbol for current is I, (I) originating from the French intensité de cou-
rant, *an intensity of electrical flow measured as a quantity per unit of time.*

Consider: we are made almost entirely of water and electricity.

So our vernacular

of emotion employs   surge

                wave   spark,

                                        impulse   and   current,

the flood of salt

                or rush of crackling

                                blue   pulse, of
                arcing rivulet.

A measurement of with and with   out.

                                        The ecstatic penetration of sperm

                into egg—
we have all seen

                                                        the microscopic

iconography.

The wombless State

                                        will ordain

this

        the electric moment of life

                              will brand each womb sanctified

        property.

My mother was conceived

        during a war waged on   brown bodies

                  and birthed

me under a moon obscured

                by flags.

                        Electric layers of ocean   reveal

            themselves as

an ancestral coding   of me and her   and her and her

                                          as the spear and the

plunge,

            the cavern of handprints

the caverns of decapitation.

The lightning spark cannot be created because it was already there.

In the gloom human nostalgia
                    presses to know   where
            when which   gods' touch

(the first impulse of light into
                                            darkness)

first enacted a separation of shadow   into meaning,

                        yet   I   fork   bead

                                    ribbon the   light

into existence insistence

        with each   sloughing

                                of salt water   blood,

        each   recollection of   current.
(I)

Tano I CHamoru.

  Our people

                              were shaped from stone

and   the
pulsing

                  sea.   .

Sister's crouched
                      body

                                          wave kneaded

      salt   lapped

          until   we tumbled
                                                    from her

of her   (of them)

                                    all strong strong   and

                        whole
                together.
        Birds
                                                                        regarded

                                                        our sea foam

        anklets

                our slippery ropes

                        of hair our

            cheeks   full
        of
                                                                        pebbles
                                and scattered from the shore

                                                                        singing.

        We opened   our new
        mouths

        to   our

                         own   chorus
crooning

        SisterBrother

we are

sun

                                    moon
        sky

                                                            water
                earth

                                                    all

                siblings.
(I)

I believe in reincarnation
                                    in so much   as

I know   an ancestor

                                    passed   to   me

the memory of

                        making   oneself

into   a universe.

                                                            One.
                                                            Self.   (I)

connected to, no—

                                    concurrent   with

            every   iteration   of

                  subatomic   movement.

How, then

              am I   queer?

                                          Queer?

Queered?

I am   also   only

                       (queer)   because
                       there is

                       a world

         outside of mine.

                                              If   the world were

only me,

I would   seem   just so.

                                              A microcosmos

             of   animal
    mineral

plant   light.

                                   Electric, I.

(I)

    Yet,   the world.

Here is what I can say:

I am   I.   Warrior, I.   Glacier, I.

         Photon, I.   Vine, I.

Rivulet, I.   Integer, I.   Summoner, I.

Wave, I.   Exhalation, I.

                    Mother, I.   Lava, I.

        Hilum, I.   Hypha, I.

                I.   I.   I.

(I)

Prism, I.   And   culture bending
            through   me.

                    The world   spits   grapples

                    tries   to tie   me up in   basements

to rid   themselves   of my   insistence.

Ancestor   wired me a path

            within.

Inside the brick spaces
throughout and becoming
the walls
                                                              and
clouds, I.

                  Swallow bolts, I   expand

I   empty   I

                  carry   within

            a hundred   thousand

wombs   of   spectacular

                                                            light.

ROBERTA HILL

Roberta Hill (also known as Roberta Hill Whiteman), Oneida, is a poet, fiction writer, essayist, and scholar whose poetry collections include *Star Quilt*, *Her Fierce Resistance*, *Philadelphia Flowers*, and *Cicadas: New and Selected Poetry*. She was a professor of English and American Indian Studies, affiliated with the Nelson Institute for Environmental Studies at the University of Wisconsin, until her retirement in May 2020. She has read her poetry internationally and currently lives and writes in the Driftless Area of Wisconsin.

Focal Flame Photography

These Rivers Remember

In these rivers, on these lakes
Bde-wa'-kan-ton-wan saw the sky.
North of here lies *Bdo-te,*
Center of the Earth. Through their songs,
the wind held onto visions.
We still help earth walk
her spiral way, feeling
the flow of rivers
and their memories of turning
and change.

Circle on circle supports us.
Beneath the tarmac and steel in St. Paul,
roots of the great wood are swelling
with an energy no one dare betray.

The white cliffs, *I-mni-za Ska,*
know the length of *Kangi Ci'stin'na's* tears.
He believed that words spoken
held truth and was driven into hunger.
Beneath the cliffs, fireflies flickered
through wide swaths of grass.
Oaks grew on savannahs, pleasant
in the summer winds where deer
remain unseen.

These rivers remember their ancient names,
Ha-ha Wa'-kpa, where people moved
in harmony thousands of years
before trade became more valuable than lives.

In their songs, the wind held
onto visions. Let's drop our burdens
and rest. Let's recognize our need
for awe. South of here, the rivers
meet and mingle. Bridges and roads,
highway signs, traffic ongoing.
Sit where there's a center
and a drum, feel the confluence
of energies enter our hearts
so their burning begins to matter.

This is *Maka coka-ya kin*,
The Center of the Earth.

CATHY TAGNAK REXFORD

Cathy Tagnak Rexford, Inupiaq, is a playwright, poet, and fiction writer from Anchorage and Kaktovik, Alaska. The author of the chapbook *Black Ice*, which appeared in *Effigies: An Anthology of New Indigenous Writing, Pacific Rim*, she currently lives and writes in Boulder, Colorado, with her husband and son.

Nadya Kwandibens, Red Works Photography

Anchorage, 1989

And now, that look on your face:
the same residue you found on
the murre eggs upriver, as if
the damp earth left its fingerprint on your
eyelids as we sat across from each other
in the café. And now, the length

of your legs just short of touching
my legs underneath the table, the memory
of the way we wrapped our limbs together,
eclipsed, like the old village on
that island where we met. And we
would relocate ourselves, or what we

thought it meant to be ourselves.
In Anchorage, when the snow cracked
beneath your feet, and the mountains
seemed a little larger than usual, you
offered your hands, opened. I remember,
not because I thought about taking them,

but because when my hands lay cupped
in yours—both browned of sun—it reminded
me of hunting caribou upriver, squinting
against sunlight, in that rock canyon.
I did take your hands, because it was polite
and you didn't mean to hold them

for more than a moment; it was the only thing
you could offer then. Now, I straighten
my silverware set on the table, as if
you might tell me what I really want to hear
which was not that we were wrong,
but that our weakness really means

that we are linked somehow with history,
the same history that has brought us
together miles from the old village
on that island where we met.
Those mornings you'd wake up first
to make coffee and listen to water fall from

the edge of the roof in the spring,
are as faint now as the smell of damp earth
beneath concrete. And I cannot look you
in the eye, because sometimes,
eye contact is more intimate than breath
in whispers, like that trip we took upriver,

when our daughter balanced on the edge
of the boat, leaning out, dragging her fingers
in the water, as meaningless now as this
meeting today in the café, listening to
our waitress swear under her breath
as she takes our order, two mugs of coffee

braided in her fingers. A gust of wind
rips through the front door of the café
when a short man in red Chuck Taylors
smiles at me as he brushes the snow from
his shoulders—the kind of man you were
before I found you resting under the

overpass of New Seward Highway this afternoon.
It was an accident finding you
there. I wanted that man standing
next to the flashing jukebox to come over, sit in
your seat and work the Sunday crossword
puzzle with me, but he didn't. And now, I

leave you, like the old village on that island
where we met, on the corner of Ingra
and 5th Avenue after you asked me
for twenty dollars, but I see now it is the same—
the aluminum boat, the murre eggs,
the coffee dripping over the lip of the mug,

the dark of your eyelids—each held
in drowned memory, the same way our mouths
know the taste of salt, or not salt itself,
but the memory of salt. It is a narrow passage
between breath and memory, leaning inward.
And according to you it wasn't our

reflexes that failed us, that day on the river
in that second she fell from the boat,
but that we were inexperienced. And now,
in the cottoned quiet of my car, a snowplow
scrapes against hard-packed snow, and
I don't know how to tell you that I need

the story to take a breath. As we told it
to strangers, suffering the quiet of
silt and current unmoving, doubting,
in the same way, if she too, lay unmoving.
I drove and I refused our directional relation,
where the only word for backward

meant stern and forward meant bow.
And I heard your voice stretching over the
curved tundra, telling me stories of swans
who took flight and fell to the earth
to become humans. It was simple then,
like the old village on that island where

we met. But, when I found you
crossing the street, you were frozen,
drunk, clutching your thermos, your clothes
stitch-marked and thinned and you looked
as though you might stand up to argue with me
about life jackets and the way the shallows

in the river had shifted those ten years before
and I would have yelled back at you to slow down,
but all that is left is the hum of my Buick
as I wait for you to cross the street,
your breath creating its own cloud formation.
And now, every time I listen to Cat

Stevens, I think of her, so I have set out
all the albums and even the record player
on the street and listen in the morning
to that snow plow that keeps me awake,
thinking of caribou hunting and winding
switchbacks under the 3 A.M. sun. It was

the way each song would sing to the next
song and would sing to lungs filled with
river water. And our voices, alone,
were not enough on the island in the old village
where we met. So I lit a cigarette,
in the early grey light of morning and kept watch.

JOY HARJO

Joy Harjo, a member of the Muscogee (Creek) Nation, is the twenty-third Poet Laureate Consultant in Poetry to the Library of Congress and the first Native American poet to serve in the position. She is the author of nine poetry collections, most recently *An American Sunrise*, and the award-winning memoir *Crazy Brave*. In 2019, she was awarded the Jackson Prize and was elected as a chancellor of the Academy of American Poets.

Shawn Miller, Library of Congress

Exile of Memory

Do not return,
We were warned by one who knows things
You will only upset the dead.
They will emerge from the spiral of little houses
Lined up in the furrows of marrow
And walk the land.
There will be no place in memory
For what they see
The highways, the houses, the stores of interlopers
Perched over the blood fields
Where the dead last stood.
And then what, you with your words
In the enemy's language,
Do you know how to make a peaceful road
Through human memory?
And what of angry ghosts of history?
Then what?

Don't look back.

In Sunday school we were told Lot's wife
Looked back and turned
To salt.
But her family wasn't leaving Paradise.
We loved our trees and waters
And the creatures and earths and skies
In that beloved place.

Those beings were our companions
Even as they fed us, cared for us.
If I turn to salt
It will be of petrified tears
From the footsteps of my relatives
As they walked west.

I did not know what I would find

The first night we set up our bed in the empty room
Of our condo above the Tennessee River
They'd heard we were coming
Those who continued to keep the land
Despite the imposition of newcomers
And the forced exile of our relatives.

All night, they welcomed us
All night, the stomp dancers
All night, the shell shakers
All night circle after circle made a spiral
To the Milky Way

We are still in mourning.

The children were stolen from these beloved lands by the government.
Their hair was cut, their toys and handmade clothes ripped
From them. They were bathed in pesticides

And now clean, given prayers in a foreign language to recite
As they were lined up to sleep alone in their army-issued cages.

Grief is killing us. Anger tormenting us. Sadness eating us with disease.
Our young women are stolen, raped and murdered.
Our young men are killed by the police, or killing themselves and each other.

This is a warning:
Heroin is a fool companion offering freedom from the gauntlet of history.
Meth speeds you past it.
Alcohol, elixir of false bravado, will take you over the edge of it.
Enough chemicals and processed craving
And you can't push away from the table.

If we pay enough, maybe we can buy ourselves back.

We used to crowd the bar for Tuesday ten-cent beer night.
It was the Indian, poetry, biker and student bar
In that university and military base town.
Trays packed with small cups of beer passed non-stop
Over the counter all night.
We brought all of our thirsty dreams there
Gambled with them at the pool table, all night.
Danced with them and each other on the blood-stained dance floor
To jukebox songs fed by dimes and quarters, all night.
And by 2 A.M. we staggered out
To the world made by Puritan dreaming

No place for Indians, poets or any others who would
Ride the wild winds for dangerous knowledge.

All night.

Here there is a singing tree.
It sings of the history of the trees here.
It sings of Monahwee who stood with his warrior friends
On the overlook staring into the new town erected
By illegal residents.
It sings of the Civil War camp, the bloodied
The self-righteous, and the forsaken.
It sings of atomic power and the rise
Of banks whose spires mark
The worship places.
The final verse is always the trees.
They will remain.

When it is time to leave this place of return,
What will we say that we found here?

From out of the mist, a form wrestles to come forth—
It is many-legged, of many arms, and sent forth thoughts of many colors.
There are deer standing near us under the parted, misted sky
As we watch, they smell for water
Green light enters their bodies
From all leaved things they eat—

The old Mvskoke laws outlawed the Christian religion
Because it divided the people.
We who are relatives of Panther, Raccoon, Deer, and the other animals
    and winds were soon divided.
But Mvskoke ways are to make relatives.
We made a relative of Jesus, gave him a Mvskoke name.

We cannot see our ancestors as we climb up
The ridge of destruction
But from the dark we sense their soft presences at the edge of our minds
And we hear their singing.

There is no word in this trade language,
No words with enough power to hold all this we have become—

We are in time. There is no time, in time.
We are in a Mvskoke village, far back in time.
Ekvnvcakv is in labor, so long in time.
She is not young and beyond the time of giving birth.
The keeper of birthing is tracking her energy, and time.
My thinking is questioning how, this time.

A young boy wrestles with two puppies at the doorway.
A little girl, bearing an old woman spirit appears
With green plants in her hands.
Twins play around the edge of the bed.

The Earth's womb tightens with the need to push.
That is all that I see because of the fogginess of time.

I sing my leaving song.
I sing it to the guardian trees, this beloved earth,
To those who stay here to care for memory.
I will sing it until the day I die.

CENTER/NORTH–SOUTH

GORDON HENRY JR.

Gordon Henry Jr., an enrolled citizen of the White Earth Anishinaabe Nation, is a poet and fiction writer. His writing has been published in numerous anthologies in the United States and has been translated into German, Spanish, Catalan, and Italian. Gordon teaches creative writing and American Indian literature in the English Department at Michigan State University.

Gordon Henry Jr.

River People—The Lost Watch

When we were river people
once in a while you talked different,
different because we were under
the influence of elders—their repetition,
a northern dialect of hands
coming apart in stories.

When we were river people
the sun made an alphabet
of light struck trees
while you sat on a stump
in the yard and rolled
tobacco from the plants
we grew
in the raised beds
by the power
pole.

When we were river people
the dog we took from dog death row
at the shelter got cancer and
we put her in the ground near
where young thunder woman
learned to hit golf balls
toward an old shirt on a stick
where every shot was lost.

When we were river people we made medicine
for Zahquod and fasted and sweat at dawn
for four days, following Eagleheart's instructions.
Zahquod drank the tea for a few months
and died the following fall.

When we were river people we put stones
in the mailbox to keep the weekend rowdies
from hitting it again while we slept
and we drove
to town every Thursday to
take Anungoonce to tap class.

There were boys after her after that
and we let one in.
There she held him close often and made sure
he got his needle before he stupored in
dropping sugar.

When we were river people
big leaf rhubarb grew,
wild Turkeys walked in the mist
up the drive
a few big hens in front
and the gas man apologized when
he saw you talking with pwaagun

early one Friday when you heard the news
about Zahquod starting on interleukin 2.

When we were river people you listened
to Townes every day for a week of summer
'to live is to fly' he said 'both low and high'
he said
he reminded you of Smoke
with his cracked hard
Oklahoma voice
the week you watched his horse
and the belly laugh his goddaughter
Anungoonce let loose
outside the barbed wire
pasture fence as Seguili the horse ran.

When we were river people we lost power
for five days one winter, so we braced
ourselves on fallen logs when we shit outside
and we fed the woodstove and slept on the
floor and drove to Canadian Lakes to shower.

When we were river people
singing woke you one night
and you ran outside asking
the stars and the creator to help
you remember the words

remember the words
Giizhay manidoo have pity
Giizhay manidoo bring healing.

When we were river people Geeshik
Eway Abaat would not talk to you
though you kept asking to let your love
for her find its way to her, so you could
tell her about the shooting star and her birth
under a formation of white cranes
And so you could laugh with her
about when she was three,
when she came crying out
of the sweat with Grandma Rose.

When we were river people visitors
came with strangers and strangers came with
friends to bring wood and stones for namings
sweats and thirsty dance sings and all those
gifts Eagleheart shared with you
when you lived out west.

When we were river people deer
ran through morning by morning
one morning a string of them
one walking wounded outside
hobbling on three legs, an arrow

through the fourth, outside the
window as you made breakfast for all
the girls who came looking for Nawgwayawp
stayed overnight after the dance.

When we were river people there was
no time for writing, too many people
were dying, too many children were
growing, there were too many ceremonies
to make, too much firewood to cut, too many calls,
too many fasts, too many trips to
White Earth and Turtle Mountain
too much burned gas
too many names requested
to be given, to people you know
who still don't know who they are,
too many appointments, disappointments,
too much tired talk, the difference between
going to sleep and staying up
already past deciding.

When we were river people
Crow knew just like you know now
a stone is no place for a watch
as you know what we call time

can't be made up with words
lost, or remembered, or held down

to earth, or be left behind
by blessings, forgotten, or be any more
than a relative of light, who returns home,
as bright clear sun reporting all
that has gone between rising and falling.

DUANE NIATUM

Duane Niatum, Jamestown S'Klallam tribe, has been writing poems, stories, and essays for more than sixty years. He is the author of ten books of poems, most recently *Earth Vowels* and the chapbook *Sea Changes*. The legends and traditions of his ancestors help shape and animate his poetry. Niatum has made a lifelong study of European and American Indian art, literature, and culture.

Marti Spencer

Old Humptulips

For my Grandfather, Francis Patsey

In the spirit of seawater,
you jump from one boulder to another,
and with the quick dip of the hand
you draw from under the next rock
a fifth sculpin, grab it by the gills,
a fish our people say sings to us,
a gift you will clean and roast on the beach fire
for your love and grandchildren.
Your new neighbors that came from the East
stare at you from outside the circle,
behind a blackberry bush, curious
yet guarded and unattached.
They have settled in the ruins of your family's
abandoned village of white fir and cedar.
They surround your crumbling longhouse
plagued with a disease no shaman understood
or could fight with rattle, smoke or song.
These settlers fear your sculpin dance
and refuse to join your family feast.
So you imagine they are grey willows
vanishing on the wind of mountain guardians,
step toward the beach, a whirling
sunspot on the sand print of strangers.

ANITA ENDREZZE

Anita Endrezze is an artist and a writer. Her most recent book of poetry, *Enigma*, was published in 2019. Anita is Yaqui, Pima, and Maya as well as half European (Slovenian, German, and Italian).

Maja Hansen

Thirteen Ways of Looking at an Indian

1

Among twenty Indians only one
has skin as coppery as a penny
and she sprayed it on.

2

If you're a half-breed,
you're always of two minds
but your heart is Red.

3

Coyote whirls in dust devils,
grinning in the heart
of our stories.

4

A man and a woman
(or a man and a man
or a woman and a woman)
are one. A human and Coyote
are trouble.

5

I don't know which I prefer:
Native American, ndn, Indian.
Skins or sly innuendos from Coyote
as he saunters down the street,
whistling, "Yo, *mamacita*, you bad honey!"

6

I grew up half white, but
Coyote's shadow is moody, dark-twin
to mine.

7

O Non-Native—ndn—injuns! Why do you exterminate
Coyote? Hang his pelt on barbed wire, string
his ears on your belts? Do you not see how Coyote
is part of this land, the dreaming and scheming
of Thought into Existence? Without Coyote
America would be a reservation of flat jokes
and fizzled life.

8

I grew up in Southern California where rivers
are cement troughs and Coyote sang from Hollywood Hills.
My aunts wouldn't say they were Yaqui
because that meant death or slavery in Sonora.
So they were Mexican with indigenous rhythm.

9

When the Conquistadors came
or the priests or the Pilgrims
or Walmart, we ran away. We ran in circles
from death in one land to death in another,
and Coyote was always there, holding our souls
in the depths of his howl.

10

At the smell of smudged sage at the powwow,
the white cop sniffed sharply, looking for some Indian
smoking weed.

11

I tried riding in a canoe and almost tipped over.
Horses scare me. My car has scars along its flanks
from spatial misjudgments as I back out of the garage.
My kind of Indian is self-defined. It's whatever I do,
however I do it. I'm not scared of who I am.

12

Fry bread is a recent tradition. Corn is older
and part of my DNA. Corn is sacred, pollen flying
into a world turned golden. Like Coyote's fur.

13

Today lasted centuries. Coyote sits next to me,
whispering promises of survival: *mañana*. It is tomorrow
and will always be tomorrow.
Stars shine all day, forever, and we don't see them.
Ours souls, whether white or ndn or Other, shine even longer.
There are more than thirteen ways of seeing anyone.

NILA NORTHSUN

nila northSun, Shoshone/Chippewa, has been writing for more than four decades and has had six books published, including *love at gunpoint*. She lives on her reservation in Fallon, Nevada.

nila northSun

i gotta be Indian tomorrow

i came back to Nevada
because somebody decided
they needed a native american
on their radio show
& i came to mind
i'm flattered
& my ego drove me
200 miles over snow packed mountains
but now
before the interview/reading
i'm panicked
i haven't written an "Indian poem"
in a long time
maybe only 1 out of 100 poems
even touch my tribal-ness
they think just because
i am native
means anything
i write somehow is rooted
in native-ness
but in flipping the pages of
my 3 ring binder
i find nothing mentioning
mother earth or feathers or reservations
even though
i stand on mother earth

& my rearview mirror has
an eagle feather tied to it
& after the interview
i'll be going back to the reservation
to see my family

is that indian enough
for them? i don't know
i guess it will have to be
tomorrow
i'll think deeper
about being indian.

BRANDY NĀLANI MCDOUGALL

Originally from Kula, Maui, Brandy Nālani McDougall is of Kanaka ʻŌiwi (Hawaiʻi, Maui, and Kauaʻi lineages), Chinese, and Scottish descent. She is the author of a poetry collection, *The Salt-Wind: Ka Makani Paʻakai*, and has edited three anthologies of poetry from the Pacific region. She also served as a contributing editor for *When the Light of the World Was Subdued, Our Songs Came Through: A Norton Anthology of Native Nations Poetry*, edited by Joy Harjo, LeAnne Howe, and Jennifer Elise Foerster.

Craig Santos Perez

This Island on which I Love You

And when, on this island on which
I love you, there is only so much land
to drive on, a few hours to encircle
in entirety, and the best of our lands
are touristed, the beaches foam-laced
with rainbowing suntan oil,
the mountains tattooed with asphalt,
pocked by telescoped domes,
hotels and luxury condos blighting
the line between ocean and sky,

I find you between the lines
of such hard edges, sitting on
the kamyo stool, a bowl of coconut,
freshly grated, at your feet.

That I hear the covert jackaling
of helicopters and jets overhead
all night through our open jalousies,
that my throat burns from the scorch
of the grenaded graves of my ancestors,
the vog that smears the Koʻolaus into a blur
of greens, that I wake to hear the grind
of you blending vegetables and fruit,
machine whirl-crunching coffee beans,
your shoulder blades channelling
ocean, a steady flux of current.

Past the guarded military testing grounds,
amphibious assault vehicles emerging
from the waves, beyond the tangles
of tarp cities lining the roads, past
the thick memory of molasses coating
the most intimate coral crevices,
by the box jellyfish congregating under
'Ole Pau and Kāloa moons, at the park
beneath the emptied trees, I come
to find you shaking five-dollar coconuts
(because this is all we have on this island),
listening to the water to guess
its sweetness and youth.

On this island on which I love you,
something of you is in the rain rippling
through the wind that make the pipes
of Waikīkī burst open, long brown
fingers of sewage stretch out
from the canal, and pesticided
tendrils flow from every ridge
out to sea, and so we stay inside
to bicker over how a plumeria tree
moves in the wind, let our daughters
ink lines like coarse rootlets
in our notebooks, crayon lines

into ladders on our walls
and sheets. Their first sentences
are sung, moonlit blowhole plumes
of sound calling pebbles to couple,
caverns to be carved, ʻuala to roll
down the hillside again, and I could
choke on this gratitude for you all.

This island is alive with love,
its storms, the cough of alchemy
expelling every parasitic thing,
teaching me to love you with
the intricacies of island knowing,
to depend on the archipelagic
spelling of you lying next to me,
our blue-screen flares their own
floating islands after our daughters
have finally fallen asleep,
to trust in the shape and curve
of your hand reaching out to hold mine
making and remaking an island our own.

CARRIE AYAGADUK OJANEN

Carrie Ayagaduk Ojanen is an Inupiaq writer from the Ugiuvamiut (King Island) tribe. She received her master's in fine arts from the University of Montana and is the author of *Roughly for the North*.

Carrie Ayagaduk Ojanen

Tiimiaq, something carried,

—for Joan Naviyuk Kane

in a book
   we read about these things
   in a book
          carved figures
aŋun, aġnaq, migiqłiq

each word I know
as a dictionary
entry
take this away
and give paper
in return

my tongue against the ink
is English
naluaġmiut
sucking in the flimsy fibers
spewing out a stumbling word
I teach them to Sinaġuk and Paniataaq
all wrong
they round the words in their small mouths
small rivers, small stones
don't pity me, they are heavy stones
but they are the small rivers
I drop the stones into

Classrooms stand between us, Aakaŋ
but their language classes taught me
how to learn from books.

The years I spent away at college
bring me back, Aakaŋ.
This is how to learn a foreign tongue
from books.

still, from a leather pouch small figures
tumble out—aŋun—perhaps aaŋauraq or iŋmi—his hood around his shoulders
aġnak—perhaps nuliaq—how tenderly her brown atigi is distinguished

atausiq qituġnaklu atausiq paniklu
one and one
tiimiaq in a small pouch, in a pocket or aġġinaq,
like portraits on my phone
in case of long separation
the ice floe shakes loose and tumbles him south
a village, elsewhere, all winter
they are remembered
just so, tenderly, the small figures,
placeholders, bringing to mind his beloved.
even now the residual tenderness
travels across the sterile page
the image of the images

of the beloved
love refracted through the making cannot be contained
in the dry clinical photo, even now,
the beloved tug patiently across the distant page
at the thread strung between their hearts
even the collection
the price of the sale
of the figures
their storage in a catalogued archive (or disposal)
cannot undo the stringing of that tenderness and memory
it strums a note familiar, but unique,
one reaching toward four
the hands that carved them to remember
and distance that memory traveled
and tugged at his heart, remain.

just so, I carry this memory with me,
of Ugiuvak, of four women and a man climbing
a steep ice cliff

and a small gathering of poets
each of us making, just so, our small figures
to be carried
what we are making cannot be undone

DENISE SWEET

Denise Sweet (Anishinaabe, White Earth) is the author of a collection of new and selected poems, *Palominos Near Tuba City*. Denise is also a First Nations organizer and worked with the Wisconsin tribes to impact Native voter turnout in 2020.

Kara Counard

Palominos Near Tuba City

In the desert of burning dreams, of armadillo and centipede,
I would call this night pitch dark back home
I would watch for any star to pass into dream song

or point of light called planet to whirl and twist like
a tiny pinwheel swallowing me to its vanishing point
Here under pewter sky with words out of breath

I chase poems down like wild mares into fenced corrals
I watch close calls with wisdom rear and kick
against the fences of good judgment.

I used to think the skies brought them home,
thundering hooves and swollen bellies, ready to spark
and fire the dry bony floor, sulfuric aroma real as rain.

But now, the horses of white lightning gallop toward me
afraid of nothing, they rush with an eye for hesitation
ready to brush up against my heart with their horse madness.

Here, it is the rider standing in the wavering heat, erect
and indisputable as a lightning rod braced in the open
I stand my ground and wait, ready to hold on for dear life.

LOUISE ERDRICH

Louise Erdrich, author of *Original Fire: Selected and New Poems*, is a poet and novelist and the owner of Birchbark Books. She is a member of the Turtle Mountain Band of Chippewa in North Dakota.

Hilary Abe

Advice to Myself

Leave the dishes.
Let the celery rot in the bottom drawer of the refrigerator
and an earthen scum harden on the kitchen floor.
Leave the black crumbs in the bottom of the toaster.
Throw the cracked bowl out and don't patch the cup.
Don't patch anything. Don't mend. Buy safety pins.
Don't even sew on a button.
Let the wind have its way, then the earth
that invades as dust and then the dead
foaming up in gray rolls underneath the couch.
Talk to them. Tell them they are welcome.
Don't keep all the pieces of the puzzles
or the doll's tiny shoes in pairs, don't worry
who uses whose toothbrush or if anything
matches, at all.
Except one word to another. Or a thought.
Pursue the authentic—decide first
what is authentic,
then go after it with all your heart.
Your heart, that place
you don't even think of cleaning out.
That closet stuffed with savage mementos.
Don't sort the paper clips from screws from saved baby teeth
or worry if we're all eating cereal for dinner
again. Don't answer the telephone, ever,
or weep over anything at all that breaks.
Pink molds will grow within those sealed cartons

in the refrigerator. Accept new forms of life
and talk to the dead
who drift in through the screened windows, who collect
patiently on the tops of food jars and books.
Recycle the mail, don't read it, don't read anything
except what destroys
the insulation between yourself and your experience
or what pulls down or what strikes at or what shatters
this ruse you call necessity.

HEID E. ERDRICH

Heid E. Erdrich's book *Little Big Bully* won a National Poetry Series award in 2019. She is Ojibwe enrolled at Turtle Mountain.

Chris Felver

Peacemaking

We long ago made a peace   —a treaty—
between enemy neighbors
like this
striped blankets   sashes worked with colored beads   animal-shaped pipe
of red stone   iron hatchets inlaid with lead designs   flutes carved to look
like a duck or goose   belts woven with colored threads   brass bells
copper water vessels   red wool   rich gifts to seal the peace

Sometimes the deal did not go down

Some wanted more   to be upheld as great men   (yes—only men)

We take your names with us to speak in honor of your greatness always
and when we ever hear your name, we will say "That is a great man you speak of"
and we will tell the stories of all the deeds you've done and how fine a figure you
made, how arrayed in fine clothes, and how many horses and how large your voice .

You get the idea

Except we had to mean it   *irreversibly*
Even though those men might have stolen   broken families   murder
or maybe it was their thieving sons we killed   even then we had to forget
and mean what we said

Imagine how hard it would be to humble ourselves to humanity
Tell their stories as if they were our brothers-fathers-kin folk   —with pride

As if just making peace with them made them relatives whose shine
shined on us

We seek your peace now
for futures we cannot gift amends
unless like this
sleep —under blankets   beads of bright creatures pollinating flowers   animals
red stone   iron   flute song   duck and goose   earth full of microbes
and minerals   sun stored to serve you   wind making light and nights cool enough
water and vessels to drink   —all once a given then a gift   future riches

You get the idea

We came in peace but left the aftermath of war like mud tracked in
messed up your carpets and ate all your bread
left milk jugs empty in the fridge and worse   much worse

Let our peace be one you can reverse
No gift can be enough—if we left you and
even gone   we keep stealing your summers   leaving just the storms
if we left you winters brutal beyond history   birds gone and bugs in tornadoes
all the fish gutted   water run off

It would be OK then   to reverse the peace we made when you were born
You do not need to hold up our names   *irreversibly*
only do not curse as you say them or

please   leave us off as relatives—
make us ancestors only   as worthy as names on paper   signs
                                        Uphold the great ones
                                and if we can't be them
                                        don't speak our names at all

HENRY REAL BIRD

Henry Real Bird, author of *Wolf Teeth*, is a rancher and educator who raises bucking horses on Yellow Leggins Creek in the Wolf Teeth Mountains. He was born and raised on the Crow Indian Reservation in the tradition of the Crow by his grandparents, Mark and Florence Real Bird, and he still speaks Crow as his primary language. He served as the Poet Laureate of Montana from 2009 to 2011.

Kevin Martini-Fuller

Thought

"Thought is like a cloud
You can see through shadow to see nothing
But you can see shadow
When it touches something you know,
Like that cloud's shadow
Touching the Wolf Teeth Mountains.
When the clouds touch the mountain's top
Or where it is high
The wind is good
When you're among the clouds
Blurred ground among fog,
You are close to He Who First Did Everything,"
Said my Grandfather Owns Painted Horse.
We are but nomads asking for nothing
But the blessings upon our Mother Earth.
We are born as someone new
So then
We have to be taught
The good from the bad.
What is good, we want you to know.
What is good, we want you to use,
In the way that you are a person.

SY HOAHWAH

Sy Hoahwah earned a master's in fine arts from the University of Arkansas and is the author of two books of poetry, most recently *Night Cradle*. He is Yapaituka Comanche and Southern Arapaho.

Isis Hoahwah

Hell's Acre

I. The Hex

Last person doctored on Hell's Acre,
was an alcoholic ex-boxer.
Supposedly, later that year, he exhumed all his dead pets
and moved out of state.

I was on Hell's Acre
because I was hexed
by looking into a broken piece of mirror
wrapped in a black silk handkerchief
placed inside my boot.

Ever since, a skeleton followed me,
always trailing so closely behind
like a friend sending me off on my way.

On the west side of the mountains, pine needles were sharper.
I heard a far-off river valley.
I heard panthers summoning rain
to hide their wedding.

The skeleton got scared and held my hand.
The skeleton held my switchblade
on our way down an ancient hog trail.
"Oh, there goes your corpse again," the skeleton lullabied.

II. Blood Money

That night, fifteenth night of the month,
the moon hesitated to rise after the sun set.

Throughout the valley, all the lost hunting arrows,
and knives sang.

I made a campfire.
The skeleton made a grave,
roasted marshmallows over this grave.
We slept at the property gate of a paper company.

I dreamed I was back in Indiahoma
with a case of Coors and all my dead cousins.
I dreamed Indiahoma was a pale star
in the rearview mirror.
I dreamed the eight-headed Mupits carried spiral keys.
I dreamed I was helping Quanah Parker move back into the Star House.
I dreamed the winged snakes came back to the sky.
I dreamed I was dreaming about Ten Bears
and how he drove his knife into his own hand
to prove an obvious point to a bluecoat.
I woke up with my hands bleeding like stigmata.

The skeleton was talking in his sleep
about mason jars filled with blood money buried in dead river mud,
about the governor of the Devil's wardrobe
drinking pop with peanuts floating in it.

I couldn't tell between the humidity and skeleton breath.
The skeleton woke up,
hanging inverted on the fence with the debris.

That damn skeleton flipped me off
when pretending to offer coffee.

After breakfast, at the first willow tree we came to,
I saw four screech owls under it
throwing their eyeballs into the air
and catching them with their eye sockets.
A fox was learning this.

Every now and then, the bones ask,
"When are we not in a dream?
. . . When are we not skeletons?"

III. Secret Origin of Esqueleto

It was Saturday
under the sign of the Siamese.
I placed a half dollar
on a crescent-moon altar of caliche clay.

The moon taken, chewed up,
then spat into an empty hand,
and rubbed in a circular motion to the left.

That's how the wilderness tends to bones.

Every time they prayed for me,
all my worn-out things turned to smoke
and rose to heaven.

Really I was nothing more
than a toothpick from somewhere or another
held in the mouth of an angel
whose name comes from the sound of shivers
it causes
running down people's spine.

A single deerfly cut across
the space of my breath, hovered close
as we both listened
to the excuse of a hundred eternities.

IV. Skeleton Says

The skeleton says we're together.
We're Siamese twins.
The skeleton thinks we're on an old style horse raid.
The skeleton put an old horse bone in its mouth
to conjure up a herd.

My Siamese twin is a boring partner
and insists beer be served in cold, beveled mugs.

I need to go back to Indiahoma.
He wants to go to Branson.

We set out on a bicycle with a banana seat.
We listen for stray dogs,
rain clouds popping their collars,
for the Comanche Moon wandering the countryside,
who's not ashamed to laugh
with someone else's blood on its teeth.

So focused on listening,
we pedal out to where
moonlight breaks like a knife blade on the silence.

V. Raid

Lighting out after Beelzebub,
chimera,
medicine.
I had business.

I climbed down a ladder of wolves
to follow unraveled entrails from an old kill.

One can read the future from such.

I took shelter in abandoned blankets
piled high in moonlight
at the border of the floating world.

During a thunderstorm, Zeus and Jesus
licked the rain off each other's hands and arms
like wild animals.
I saw their connection.

The skeleton confided in me and said,
The two things you do best
are keeping me from dying and telling scary stories . . .

Then we cut through the Ozarks
like cicadas released by the breath of a vampire.

JOAN NAVIYUK KANE

Joan Naviyuk Kane's eight books of poetry and prose include the forthcoming *Dark Traffic*. She has received a Guggenheim Fellowship, the American Book Award, the Donald Hall Prize for Poetry, and a Whiting Award. She teaches in the Department of Studies in Race, Colonialism, and Diaspora at Tufts University and also teaches poetry and creative nonfiction at the Institute of American Indian Arts and at Harvard University. Kane is Inupiaq from the King Island Native Community.

Jenny Irene Miller

Rookeries

All men knew a secret of the northern part
of an old world, a less perfect

idea. For the bicornuate woman,
it was an island. Though its birds

lose our trust, we might learn
their language. After all, we have
been taught
                 to read and write,
to remove our hands
                     from other work
as we watch water twist into rock:

to cover our wounds,
staying alive light after light.

For something, I worry.

The moon pronounced with clarity
its known topography. Our letters

and lists, reconstructed grammars:
they replace the ways in which we were

grabbed, and pushed, then shoved.
Set a wife and her children

to rove with indefinite orders:

lineal migration on a small scale
is not nautical, but conflictual.

      Of those men,
we knew I could never do

them any good. In this way
I forget, and let the wind

river. It gales and tears
at my shoulders and wrists.

M. L. SMOKER

M. L. Smoker is a citizen of the Fort Peck Assiniboine and Sioux Tribes. Her family's home is on Tabexa Wakpa. She is the author of a collection of poetry, *Another Attempt at Rescue*. She earned an Emmy for her work on the PBS documentary *Indian Relay* and in 2019 she was named to a two-year term as one of two poets laureate for the state of Montana.

Dean Davis

The Book of the Missing, Murdered and Indigenous—Chapter 1

For Natalie Smoker

The winding cord of highways, unkempt
gravel roads and the trails of animals—
a record of who and what has passed over,
an agony of secrets.

In the end, they have all borne witness,
eyes like glass beads that can never blink.
The dull light of motel neon shines ominously.
An engine growls across the landscape.

Brittle men who are splintered like glass
thrown from a second story window
and we are the room they leave behind.
They are pathetic husks, feeble in spirit.

Fragments fall along fields and shallow ditches,
in overlooked alleyways or underpasses.
A cold, empty breeze rising from the debris.
The first and last moment of her.

It is rage that pulls her up from this place.
She spews out the wretched and miserable
as particles of dawn-lit soil illuminate her skin.
Her hair is a two-edged sword.

She stitches together the collective story of origin,
her body a map: descended from the stars,
on the backs of animal sisters,
carried to safety in a bird's beak.

TANAYA WINDER

Tanaya Winder is a writer, educator, and motivational speaker. She is the author of *Words Like Love* and *Why Storms Are Named After People and Bullets Remain Nameless*. Winder is Duckwater Shoshone, Pyramid Lake Paiute, and Southern Ute.

Viki Eagle

like any good indian woman

i pull my brothers from words, *stupid injun*, shot like bullets. when people ask why my brothers hated school i say: the spirit remembers what it's like to be left behind when america took children from homes, displaced families with rupture, ripping a child's hand from a mother's to put them in boarding school buildings. my brothers are mourning a loss they try to fix in finding home in another person, so they travel from reservation to city singing blues and 49 songs about love.

       i pull my brothers from cars named after indians: *navajo, cherokee,* & *tacoma.* on a danger destined road my brothers are born longing for a way back from relocation & long walks across miles & miles & miles of removal. my brothers search for themselves in unhealthy addictions disguised as makeshift bandages.

      i pull my brothers from bottles they think answers might be hidden at the bottom of. my brothers stumble through back alleys looking for a love & laughter that was stolen from them like the land. and when their brown bodies try to find healing & love, other brown bodies cringe at their touch because like any good indian woman, our bodies are connected to an earth, still being raped by the pipelines forcibly laid down inside all that we hold sacred. and my brothers hold onto their colonial emotional baggage so tightly they think it's gravity

      so i pull my brothers from oceans believing they deserve the hurt so much they nearly drown themselves in it. and sometimes my brothers knife ancestral grieving onto their wrists, slits to remember the only time we are ever red, skinned is when blood flows from the open wounds america knifed onto our brown skin. self-love: apply pressure.

i pull my brothers
from ashes. america tried to burn us not knowing we were already flame.

& these will be the stories i tell my grandchildren when one day, they
ask me—why being a good indian woman means we burn like phoenix
repeatedly pulling our brothers.

KIMBERLY BLAESER

Kimberly Blaeser, former Wisconsin poet laureate, is the author of five poetry collections—most recently *Copper Yearning, Apprenticed to Justice*, and the bilingual *Résister en dansant/Ikwe-nimi: Dancing Resistance*—and editor of *Traces in Blood, Bone, and Stone: Contemporary Ojibwe Poetry*. Anishinaabe from White Earth Reservation, Blaeser is a professor at the University of Wisconsin–Milwaukee and a faculty member in the Master of Fine Arts program at the Institute of American Indian Arts.

John Fisher

Poem on Disappearance

Beginning with our continent, draw 1491:
each mountain, compass point Indigenous;
trace trade routes, languages, seasonal migrations—
don't become attached.
Yes, reshape by discovery,   displacement
move your pencil point quickly now as if pursued—
a cavalry of possession that erases
homelands: we shrink shrink—in time-lapse
of colonial barter . . . disappear   .

Now draw a brown face painted for ceremony,
half a face, nothing

          .

Draw nothing around a crumbled bird body—
no wings.

Draw emptiness inside desecrated burial mounds,
a stretch of absence where fallopian tubes once curved in hope
sketch void across buffalo prairie, draw the empty
of elk, of passenger pigeons, of silver trout.

Conjure with your hand the shape of girl
blooming, curves of face, her laughing eyes;
you've seen them postered and amber-alerted—
missing, missing, evening newsed, and gone.

Draw a woman wrapped in a blanket
a child's body weighted—draw stones
sinking into every river on the map.

Draw carrion blackening skies, carrion
plucking vision from round brown faces
draw missing, draw murdered.

Work carefully now
turn your hand to the new continent.
Again picture it—

                         nothing   .

MAHEALANI PEREZ-WENDT

Mahealani Perez-Wendt, Kanaka Maoli (indigenous Hawaiian), directed an indigenous rights law firm in Hawaiʻi for thirty-two years. She has published poetry and short stories and is the author of *Uluhaimalama*. She and her husband, Ed, are taro farmers on his family's ancestral lands in Wailuanui, East Maui.

Kaehukai Broadhurst

Na Wai Eā, The Freed Waters

A Story of the People
of Koʻolau Moku, Maui Hikina

1. Mahiʻai Kalo, Taro Farmer

All his life loving earth
  a living harrow waist deep in mud
planting tilling trenching shoveling plowing
  mud to field, gravel to path, stones to bank
yoked no less than animal to plow
  a year of this then *huki ʻai*, harvest
shouldering the heavy bags
  heaving lifting hauling slogging
through acres of taro fields
  ancient footpaths fragile *ʻauwai* wetlands
swollen feet hands torqued elbows knees
  pestilences infestations droughts
year after year, year after year
  for love of family love of ancestors
love of the Elder Brother
  for love of *Hāloa.*

2. Loʻi Kalo, Taro Fields

As far as eye could see their green hearts
  were laid bare under rains
that never ceased falling a much aggrieved sun

the dim glint of it through upstart clouds
but always the rains and he was glad for the gods'
        beneficence and the harbingers who coaxed
sunlight's bright threads the *'auku'u* herons hovering
        then ensconced in pools
of watery green expanse their emanations of light
        vectoring the same paths trod
the same earth the same ancient waterways
        the ancestors walked he regarded the plants
hungrily the same green ones whose presentiments
        were his Elder Brother *Hāloanakalaukapalili*
vivified who was born of the gods
        Wākea and *Ho'ohōkūokalani* their union
a conflagration of heaven and brightening stars
        their firstborn, the Elder Brother
stillborn buried Ho'ohōkūokalani's tears unceasing
        until the quickening
shimmer of green in graven earth
        the unfurling leaves
and the risen Hāloanakalaukapalili
        progenitor
his offspring the stalwart green-hearted ones
        who followed growing up
out of the same earth again and again
        he called them *koa*, warriors
as they hoisted their green banners

forming leaf arbors under sun's radiance
their stems rooted deep their arbors
     protecting parents, grandparents, the corm, *mākua*
protecting children grandchildren, *'ohā*, the offshoots
     succouring cradling them
millennia of generations turning returning
     e huli, e huli, e huli ho'i, the ancestors called
their names auspicious names naming
     their offspring in dreams
through keen observations
     ho'ailona, signs
close attentions to minutiae of corm
     stem petiole rhizome
shimmering sun wind
     sea clouds and earth
cradle of the hallowed ancestors
     and the risen Hāloa
give us the right names the mākua prayed
     dispatched their entreaties released them
mana ulu, mana 'ōpelu, mana weo,
     mana uliuli, mana 'ula'ula, moi, piko,
lehua, ha'akea, hapa hapapū
     were names given
and many more all his life
     he knew and never forgot
their names

sacred from the first
they were the names of the generations
of his Elder Brother
they were the names of his family
they were the names of kalo.

3. Maka'ala, Be Vigilant

Elena his grandmother James and Samson
the grandfathers who brought him to the gods
he followed along the ancient paths
of well-tended fields
the rows of plants who were offshoots
of his Elder Brother green sentinels
as far as eye could see
he sloshed through the maze of waterways
the irreproachable fretwork of ancestors
arrayed he heard
their songs prayers incantations
traceries of winds waters ocean
he heard *Pahulena* the grandmother's birthplace
she said her birthplace name
and motioned toward a dense growth
of *'ōlena* and the tall stand of *niu*
where *'ehukai* breezes warmed
the wide river mouth churning

above reddish brown sheen of seaweed *limu kohu*
    spawning place of *āholehole, moi, ʻanae,*
pāpio, ʻoʻopu, hīhīwai, poʻopaʻa
    ʻopihi, wana, hāʻukeʻuke, ʻaʻama
he remembered stories fishing canoes divers their nets
    the surround of *akule, halalū,* mishaps at sea
the *kilo iʻa,* fish spotter's lair high above the *kāheka*
    the first catch offered there at the *ahu*
he remembered his grandmother's warning
    makaʻala and that after the bosses came
aia nō iā haʻi nā ʻāina o mākou she said
    other men have our lands
then her words went dry
    and Pahulena was no more.

4. Waimaka, Tears

There are hidden places
    where the high waters fall
in rainbowed silence
    sucked in through igneous stone
pulsing the columnar dikes
    of earth's vast waterworks
spilling over soul's sacred edge
    Elena's tears Elena's tears.

5. Naʻaupō, Ones Devoid of Light

From sea dregs the onslaught winds
    its shifting stars, the detritus tides
carry dark strangers
    under cover of night
stealthy ones of fervent prayers
    and exhortations Holy Father
bring us safely to the village
    Pahulena in the distance
grant us safe conduct
    in our sacred mission
to save the unbelievers
    for Your greater glory
Amen.
    he malihini lākou no ka ʻāina ē
ka ʻāina huna wai no Kāne
    strangers they come
to this land of hidden waters
    belonging to Kāne
ghosts grey as gunmetal
    intractable as cannons
sulphurous gunpowder flashes
    their lodestars
at artillery's first report
    the stalwart sons and daughters of Hāloa
rout the shadowy ones

but from dregs of darkness
there is no surcease
        wave upon unending wave
commend ravening spirits
        to the tasks set before them
conversions appropriations
        decimations subjugations
as has been foretold
        in their writs
they look upon Hāloa's people
        as pitiable idolaters unclean ones
who must be brought to the One God
        and called to atone
from the lost souls' darkness withal
        a Savior shall lead them
their dark paths made light
        the Savior's blood sacrifice
upon Golgotha's mouldering cross
        their lamp of redemption
na'aupō look with dismay
        upon the god *Lono*'s handiwork
his raft of green mountains
        his canopies of forest
they judge these iniquity
        evil fruit of indolence
an affront and mortification
        to industry

they are disdainful
      of Kāne, his Living Waters
flowering to sea
      abased are the natives
of this extravagant land
      upon their stolid ramparts
naʻaupō recite oaths
      their kingdom come
their will be done
      they issue the edicts
dispatch the cadres
      to bulldoze the lands
build fantastic scaffolding
      engineering marvels, masterworks
for excavation of the high mountains
      extraction of waters
to bring the vile gods low
      to siphon off the lifeblood
from the green realms
      of the Elder Brother
the brooding altars are abandoned
      the disconsolate moon holds no sway
as the waters are wastreled
      the fate of an unrighteous people
turned in dark hands
      through a marvel of gravity flow

the waters are extricated
    hoʻohemahema, i ʻō i ʻaneʻi
dug here, trenched there
    tunneled here, siphoned there
the uplands turned into wallows
    ʻinu ihu puaʻa
for dirty snouted pigs
    loosed upon the land
rooting here looting there
    through gross machinations
the sacred is harried in ungodly ways
    ditches pipes channels
tunnels siphons flumes
    aqueducts intakes funnels
dark grasping hands
    leering lewd imaginings
broad hillsides of waving cane
    the far distant and arid plains
prolific with cane tassels under brightening sun
    all of this has been foretold
all has been readied, all paths cleared
    the export tariffs have been lifted
foreign labor contracts signed
    the people's protestations—
the devil take them!
    the necessary approvals have been given

government officials are aboard
　　　　the false idols *Kū, Kāne, Lono,*
Kānaloa a me mau
　　　　banished to the greater glory
of Almighty God!

6. *The Fisher of Men*

From high promontories
　　　　elevated stations of the cross
the bosses offer prayers
　　　　for the blessing of verdant lands
mahi'ai in the fields
　　　　lawai'a at the nets
and there are remembrances
　　　　vague recollections
of One Other
　　　　a Fisher of Men who once led them
who fed multitudes
　　　　with few fish and loaves
the bosses remonstrate with themselves
　　　　as the tableau of *kua'āina*
unfolds in the lowlands
　　　　a childlike people easily duped
to be cajoled lured away
　　　　or forcibly removed

from the greening hills
            what do they know these unwitting
of the true faith, divine purpose
            the higher reckonings
of true believers
            little do they know
of theft treachery genocide
            deception stealth coercion
the idolators must be readied
            for the benefactions of civilization
naʻaupō are filled with saccharine thoughts
            of panoramic cane
the lands' expeditious acquisition
            a foregone conclusion
the unrighteous ones' swift conversion
            to a penitent upright people
the gift of civilization
            a bargain more than fair
promised by the One God
            who from the time of Adam
conferred to His true believers
            dominion over the world
these truths being self-evident
            the bosses are feverish
with thoughts of unholy war
            upon *nā kuaʻāina* the people, their gods.

7. Naming the Waters

I ka wao nahele
        in the god-realms of *Ko ʻolau*
ka ʻĀina i ka Wai a Kāne
        the lands of the waters of Kāne
the sons and daughters of Hāloa
        named the waters:
where the long waters fell seaward
        ravishing black stones
where the eyes smarted from backspray
        and in dark depths like stars
the seed pearl oysters
        their faint songs could be heard
the name *Makapipi* was given;
        where *wī, hīhīwai* shells
migrated upstream and down;
        where *wī* groves
grew as thickets
        seeding the lands
where *wī* wind sounds were heard
        the name *Hanawī* was given;
where the waters scudded cloud-like
        as though firmament
where a red sheen was seen above
        signifying the presence of Sacred Ones
the name *Kaʻaʻula* was given;

where the *mo'o* goddess
was well-pleased
    and smiled at her own reflection
in the shadow waters
    the name *Waia'aka* was given;
where limestone beds
    of *'āko'ako'a* formed
and the *ulu maika* stones were shaped
    the name *Pa'akea* was given;
the narrow-necked gourds
    for water-carrying
gave *Waiohue* its name;
    ravaneous Kamapua'a
the pig god
    his stampeding hordes
gave *Pua'aka'a* its name;
    where *wauke* was kneaded
to kapa of fine transparency
    stained with *'akala* berries
for a red birth gift
    Kōpili'ula was the name given;
where two waters converged
    and *'o'opu* scaled waterfalls
where Pele's sister the sorceress
    Kapōma'ilele removed her genitals
sent them flying to thwart
    the rutting pig god Kamapua'a

his lust for Pele
     Wailua-Iki was the name given;
where *Kane-i-ka-Pahu-Wai*
     Kane of the Great Water Source
where he was seen in the heavenly clouds
     in the verdant mountainward ridges
where he was seen in the red-tinged rainbow
     where he was rain, lightning flashes
where he slept in the glowing light
     where his great heart was heard
in the thundering waterfalls
     cascading stones quaking corals
where kalo was planted along the high ridges
     where it was planted in the wide valleys
where it was planted inland of the teeming shores
     kaulana nā ʻāina kalo
a na hoaʻāina
     where famous were the kalo lands
and the people who cultivated them
     Wailua-Nui was the name given;
where the gods *Kāne* and *Kanaloa*
     refreshed themselves in springs
near groves of red and yellow lehua
     ʻŌhiʻa was the name given;
where the stout-stemmed *olonā* grew
     where in frigid waters the strands
were immersed cured

braided into fine white cordage
for canoe lashings, fishing lines, nets
       where it was plaited
for chiefly raiment *ʻahuʻula,*
       kahili, lei, mahiʻole
where the stout-stemmed *ōlona* grew
       Waiʻanu was the name given;
where fine-grained *milo*
       were shade trees for the old chiefs
where windstorms incised the heartwood
       the omens carved into god likenesses
made into canoe paddles, serving bowls,
       implements for planting
where prolific headwaters
       were called *moana*
the name *Waiokamilo* was given;
       where *maiʻa* was food curative unguent
where its broad-leaf canopies
       were rain-coverings, enclosures
where spring waters bubbled up
       through igneous cinder, *ʻākeke*
the name *Palauhulu* was given;
       sentience along the high ridges
an exhilaration of climbing, of mounting
       gave *Piʻinaʻau* its name;
where thundering rains
       poured down hollows caves ravines

where the tumult echoed down ridges
   sidewise along boulder-strewn sea cliffs
where earth shuddered and heaved
   with *nū* sounds
where great schools of fish hearkened
   where the torrents narrowed
Nūʻāilua was the name given;
   where the torrents were made wide
Honomanū was the name given;
   where *hāpuʻu, ʻāmauʻu, hala, ʻōhe,*
niu, loulu, kī, halapepe, ulu
   where *mamaki, ʻiliʻahi, wiliwili,*
koa, palapalai, palaʻa
   where *kukui, hau, milo, kamani, awa*
where cherished forest plants grew
   the name *Punalau* was given;
where *tapa*-beating logs were harvested
   the black and red berries
stained for dyes
   the name *Kōlea* was given;
where a glowing light appeared
   above the ridgeline
signifying the presence of *Kāne*
   the name *Haʻipuaʻena* was given;
where in cold springs
   aliʻi wāhine bathed
the name *Waiakamōʻī* was given;

where the aliʻi wāhine ran
to the flat hiding stone
where she found refuge
from the pig god Kamapuaʻa
the name *Wahinepeʻe* was given;
no ka mea, he mau inoa akua lākou
e ola nō lākou a pau.
in the god-inspired naming
the people remembered
because they remembered
the waters lived.

8. Koʻolau, *The Windward Cliffs*

All night
and for endless days like ghost canoes
at full sail under brightening moon
the billowing ʻĪʻaleʻale winds sweep across
Koʻolau mountain seacliffs
over razor edged ridges valleys
with thunderous bursts exhalations
obscurations of light
the spectral crew worrying each blade leaf
branch with roaring cascades waterfalls
avalanches rockslides incessant rains
it is the season of *hoʻoilo*

hoʻīloli ke kai, the sea rages
> the god Kanaloa furious his seamounts shaking

he hurls himself against seacliffs
> sending ʻaʻama scuttling over the reefs

shoals corals the staid seaweed
> *limu wawaiʻiole, limu manauea, limu ʻeleʻele,*

limu kohu, limu huluhuluwaena
> their swaying frondescences under frothy waves

in the uplands kalo
> revel in watery pools

rainbows bead on the leaf-green
> arbors of scintillate light

refractions mirrored prisms riven
> by Kane-i-ka-Wai-Ola

Kāne takes the form of a night owl
> he thrusts his wings and talons

disarming his enemies
> Kāne god of the living waters

walks abroad with Lono
> scion of water, scion of land together

summoning forth the sacred springs *Oiana!*
> waters gush forth out of earth

the living waters of Kāne coursing to sea.

DEPARTURE/WEST

KIM SHUCK

Kim Shuck is the author of seven books, including *Deer Trails*. She is also the seventh poet laureate of San Francisco and a member of the Cherokee Nation of Oklahoma.

Doug Salin Photography

This River

Runs west and
Counter to every story I drank
Deep in those small doll days
Strange, heavy with collective
Unconscious with all of those
West running, improbable relations spending
Lavish hands worth of emotion on this imagined
West in this city which also
Runs west into an ocean that I
Own no stories for, borrowed ocean full of
Marvels fed by these long men who collect different
Water who polish stones that won't tell me the
Future in any language I know

ALEX JACOBS

Alex Jacobs, author of *Loving . . . in the Reagan Era* and *This Is a Terrorist Act*, is a Mohawk visual artist, spoken-word poet, and freelance writer based on the Saint Regis Mohawk Territory on the border between New York and Canada. He lived in Santa Fe, New Mexico, for twenty-seven years, and he travels there to work on art and poetry projects and to attend Indian art markets.

Alex Jacobs

Trudell

I know, I know, I been there
I feel it, I felt it, I been there
I'm scared; I'm scared of what I saw
Scared of what I felt, scared of my thoughts
Scared of knowledge, scared of wisdom
Scared of my ignorance, scared of my arrogance
      I'm scared of my life
But I'm strong, strong for my son, strong for my daughter
I'm strong for my mom, she seen it all
I'm strong for my dad, worked himself to death
I'm strong for my loves, all these beautiful women
Who knew me better than I knew my self.
I'm strong for my people, who have been captured, killed,
Put away, tortured, brainwashed, left out to dry.
Strong for my people who think I'm crazy
Strong for my people who can't see the light no more
Strong for my people who fight every day
Strong for my people who will die far away from home
Strong for the sell-outs, the doubters, the vanished
The banished, the incarcerated, the cancerated, the polluted,
The chronic, the addicted, the consumerated, the consumed.
I'm strong for the traditional, the rational, the practical, the political.
I'm strong for my people who have given up
I'm strong for my people who have been beaten down
I'm strong for my people who have turned their lives around
I'm strong for my people who only care about things
And turned their lives into GNPs CODs ATMs MIAs MFAs

Degrees of disconnection, financial portfolios instead of dreams,
Visions of power replaced by coercion, corruption and greed.
As long as the money flows and the casino tables are green
As long as they think history can never be repeated
As long as they never read the signs or open their eyes
Or listen to elders who hear the earth cry
As long as they allow their own children to become
Indoctrinated by a system that is built on lies.

> I want to be strong, strong again
> I want to be strong, strong again
> But I'm scared, scared for my life
> But I'm strong, strong again
> Thank you
> Thank you, John . . .

B: WILLIAM BEARHART

b: william bearhart is a direct descendant of the St. Croix Chippewa Indians of Wisconsin. He was a graduate of the Lo Rez MFA program at the Institute of American Indian Arts and was a poker dealer in a small Wisconsin casino when he was not writing or editing. His work can be found in *Boston Review, North American Review, Prairie Schooner,* and *Tupelo Quarterly,* among others. He died in 2020 during the production of *Living Nations, Living Words*; his work endures in this collection of living poets.

Thomas Lindfors

Transplant:
After Georgia O'Keeffe's *Pelvis IV*, 1944
for that 26-year-old in Florida

Wolves have two stomachs, I only have one
Inside their den, regurgitation of skeleton and then another

There is quiet now in our hospital rooms
Ventilator's tail pulled from electrical socket

Parents weep a lake. A sky and moon, too
They weep a pelvis. It hangs in a museum

I steal your hip bone, tuck it deep inside my pocket
Where else does a love note fit if not next to a groin

The hip's eye blue nests a moon
I disguise myself from God

Black robed messenger, two buzzards fight for a kidney
Your mother writes *He never met a stranger*

O'Keeffe in the desert, her pilgrimage, a transplant
Long after the buzzards and wolves have left

Two pictures of your strangerless face in the post
Two blue eyes, spring starflowers harvested from God's garden

Organs reaped from a body I didn't sow
Such porcelain gifts a fragile body sows

I ingest dissolvable moons so that we become strangers
Two skeletons of different stomachs:

One lost in the desert, the other a planet, a god
A wolf swallows his own rib to rebuild all of us

MARCIE RENDON

Marcie Rendon, author of *Dreaming into Being*, is a White Earth Nation Anishinaabe author, playwright, poet, and community arts activist.

Jaida Grey Eagle

Resilience

My mother, in 7th grade, ran from a South Dakota boarding school
back home to White Earth in an age before Interstate highways, cell
phones or google maps. That determination and love of life is resilience.
A Native father sitting in Perkins, after working a late shift, with a
two-year-old toddler in a high-chair. Explains that the baby's mother
showed up at his door with a child he didn't know existed and said,
"Here, I've done this for two years, I'm done. He's yours." He didn't
hesitate to do the right thing. That is resilience.

The woman who lost her child to child protection because she was
caught in the cycle of addiction and street life. Sent to prison. Who
spent five years getting clean, going to meetings, petitioning the court
against all odds to regain custody of her child. That is resilience.

The poet, who grew up with a not-so-easy life in Oklahoma. Resilience
gave her words to write, now US poet laureate. Resilience also gave her
music in her heart that pours out of her saxophone, healing hearts of
listeners.

A Native Artist living on the street collected discarded lipstick and
eyeshadow to create gallery-worthy paintings. Creating beauty out of
beauty-discards. That is resilience.

My father, along with thousands of other fathers, for more generations
than we want to remember, sat alone, not changing residence, waiting,
waiting, waiting for children to return. That is resilience.

Men who went to prison—who somehow came out and started
businesses, who raised families and took jobs way below their skill level;
who became sweat lodge runners, sun dancers and pipe carriers. That is
resilience.

The children, raised in families outside the culture, who followed their heart's spirit back home—facing rejection, ridicule, identity-questioning—but staying, becoming one with the community, one with their tribe. That is resilience.

Mothers—who, with or without shame, have stood in line at Salvation Army for cheap toy giveaways, food shelf lines, who sit in welfare offices again and again because it is one way to keep the family going. That is resilience.

Our relatives who never hesitate to go to war, wars that are never ours. Code talkers, tunnel rats, snipers, those who walk point, medics. They die fighting because that is what we do. Or they come home and hide the pain as best they can and carry flags at Grand Entry. Or not. That is resilience.

People who give more than they get. Mothers who love their children, fathers who stay. Grandparents who babysit, even in a wheelchair.

We create beauty out of scraps. Hold cars together with duct tape. Work jobs and sell beadwork for cash to 'have a little extra.' Make frybread even though we know it isn't good for the diabetes but because it's good for the spirit.

Resilience is making decisions that benefit the whole instead of just the individual. It is getting up and putting one foot in front of the other, even when you don't want to. This is our resilience.

JOE DALE TATE NEVAQUAYA

Joe Dale Tate Nevaquaya (Comanche/Yuchi) is a longtime visual artist and poet. His poetry collection *Leaving Holes and Selected New Writings* won the prestigious Oklahoma Book Award for Poetry in 2012.

Vicki Monks

In the Field

In the field
on the Poet's
visions of earth that began
their machine romance
our dreams epidemic hearts beat
fueled a little faster.
where in the fossils world they're released

On a rainy winter day
you dream
of a sense of dislocation
murmuring
secrets of wind like rivers through murky waters—tinted
tealike by
the mangroves

The way you described Geographica Power of Light
archivists of flame
at home among
Silvery ghosts at twilight,
Swim in circles, bump one another, turn, and fly the other way.

Stand still,
Watch rattled windows captures the plume
twenty miles away

Transformed its snow into Night Salt

One language
humming the words
down from the summer
the sprawling river are glorious
color and the season
the vibrancy of the apricot
silhouetted against trees on the surface. Beneath
palette are reflected in the singular
have a textural sensibility

Fires burning
Think of the fall without your interior world
Remembering this gift from the stars
Grows in the sun and mirrored
Surfaces were everywhere
Where form word is "topography"

Ghostly in the gaunt
Shadows on wheat fields
Dwarfed splendor
Architects of the graffiti of isolation
A grist
Glacial calling Incandescent
Fastness of the Frozen archive of
Resonance

Climatic and mysterious
The secret of our Quiet
Oasis in the stone
Rises mushroom in the old
Names of rivers—
1,500 years of winter in the
Heart
Minimal lights, that mumbles saffron
Dwellers
And breathe in the ephemeral
Hungry for a thousand years

Felt
House in mind put on this earth
Surrounded by darkness,
bayous of
bone or teeth are exposed,
(185 miles) north of
Witness
Articulate speech
tumbling down
as a cloth
unwinding marionette lines
protecting
eyes of the weird
pushes out of reservoir
far as the door

indeed
mysteries do lie
alone as the most
of the unknown. Quickly hardened
of heart to it
was extracted

beamed ceilings and latticed
library of pollen
north-pointing
in the light shirt,
to sea in late Nietzsche autumn
Residence at the rainy season
creaks plain black dust
arc of an early
Harp
effects
pied territories
of the morning trench
sands are locked
by the wind
Dark purple
subterranean
pools of rain—
switches to south,
blue accents
in the rest

white pine in a distressed
arabesque horse on the mural. Antique weathervanes
mapped from the air,
restoration hard
sustenance as the night-fields'
spills (left) from a high cirque once
when one is never
filled with glacial ice. From the past new and
discontinued
Summer meltwater
Of Trapridge Glacier and feather quills—were
Natural pauses
Seen in rock

Remote runs the
Days of sieving Sea Smoke
The balance is harmonious
Where we stood went
Glories of the crow's feet
Still absent were coarse salt
Fine lines
of tobacco and a dab of burnt apricot
blue with accents
of the tea paper on the ceiling of the earliest higher
excavated light
abducted grasping
the Old World made of resin, clocks. Cross the old creek

over the years
loose soil
white ironstone.
intensifies the shimmer
counterpoint
together to glimpse
astonish with stone
of wild back into ceremony
Hence the reasoning

Peering into landscapes in motion are common lunettes with foliate filling
winds, providing winter
scree riding a submerged ice core
and thus winter
glacier's foot.
In the left ear a silver-colored falconry glove
brings the snow
the seas
with electric thermometers key in a season
of light and form
bask
carved tulips and salmon red music—and breathe deeply
as interior ice presses
home to great blue
Fire & Light Origin

NO'U REVILLA

No'u Revilla, author of *Permission to Make Digging Sounds*, is a queer 'Ōiwi poet, educator, and aloha 'āina. She has performed and facilitated workshops throughout Hawai'i as well as in Canada and Papua New Guinea and at the United Nations. She is proud to have taught poetry at Pu'uhuluhulu University, a Hawaiian place of learning established at Pu'uhonua o Pu'uhuluhulu on Hawai'i island, while standing with her lāhui, or nation, to protect their sacred mountain Maunakea in the summer of 2019.

Bryan Kamaoli Kuwada

Shapeshifters Banned, Censored, or Otherwise Shit-Listed, aka Chosen Family Poem

The one whose ma'i was stolen as she slept.

The one who sold everything to live as bite marks.

The one named Mai, Mai, E 'Ai.

The one raising his scalp like foil from a pan of meat.
    You know how many pigs I've killed, he asks.
    And when he says *kill* he means it affectionately.
    Not *I killed pigs to feed my blood* but *I slept with pigs,*
    my arms hooked around them.
    When you love what you kill.

The one who thinks he knows who stole the ma'i.

The one with 'ō'ō feathers instead of hair. The years it took to catch each
    bird and adorn her head in yellow.

The one swallowing a kukui tree for the rest of her life.

The one who became the rest of her life.

The one still searching for the ma'i.

The one meant to be a locked door but fell in love with the crank of
    keys. *I'd rather hear that sound and die*, she said.
    Now all the doors in Kahului stay open.

The one made of open until her drunk mother chased her with a knife
    screaming *you filthy, you filthy, you filthy fucking broad.*
    She is the cure to everything that hurts but will never let anyone
    touch her again.

The one growing into long, solid sticks to poke at women who, after
    kissing another woman for the first time, do not speak for days.
    In the grove in Hā'ō'ū, they plant their tongues.

The one who slept with the maʻi first.
The one who slept with the maʻi last.
The one currently sleeping with the maʻi because
maʻi was never stolen.
The one all-remembering, coughing up coconuts as she laughs.
Sometimes they call her grove. Sometimes, Hāʻōʻū.

TIFFANY MIDGE

Tiffany Midge is an enrolled citizen of the Standing Rock Sioux Tribe and was raised in the Pacific Northwest. She is an award-winning poet and writes humor essays, fiction, and memoir. She is the author of the books *Bury My Heart at Chuck E. Cheese's* and *The Woman Who Married a Bear*.

Jay Dearien

Antiquing with Indians

First it was the tumblers for highballs—
cocktail hour with primitives,
the kind your grandma used to wear her red dress for.

$30 seemed too steep, even for a stereotype,
even for bones, perfect and white, snapped through
afros, pierced through noses, prehistoric as flint.

Still you wanted them, even if you don't drink
anymore. Then it was the Battle of Little Bighorn
board game, replete with war-bonneted Sioux

and Cheyenne, action figures on horseback;
plastic Gatling guns and cannons,
tomahawks and war shields galore.

But you're above all that. Except for the beaded Indian
doll, the pin cushion with a wrist clasp—
you want to be that Indian wearing the Indian

like a Russian doll, you want to uncover
and uncover, go undercover and pin yourself
back to completion again; buy the beaded skirt

for those days when Voodoo seems a viable option
(you know the ones). Just as we'd brisked
through the door, the real-life doll version

of Pocahontas and John Smith (what a pair!)
a voice from the back called out . . . *squaw man* . . .
later we found the 1906 novel the voice was referring.

Don't you want to be more than a metaphor?
That's the beauty of it, that's the trick,
you think ironies are free, but they're not.

Latona mentioned how she'd discovered
a Tonto doll, stoic and monosyllabic,
seated next to a Custer puppet

which had so unnerved her she felt it her duty
to relocate Tonto to a more auspicious corner—
someplace safe next to doilies or Fiestaware.

What wars might emerge from such proximity
she'd wondered. What skirmishes could result?
I imagined the Iroquois Brave

brandished on the alfalfa seed cloth sack
could overtake the Yakama Squaw Apple box
succeed his throne beyond the Calumet Baking Powder's

proud profile. Don't mess with vintage
the collections seemed to warn. If you think
this is Toy Story, you got another thing coming.

ERIC GANSWORTH

Eric Gansworth, S'ha-weñ na-saeˀ, is a writer and visual artist, and a citizen of the Onondaga Nation, raised at Tuscarora Nation. His work, including *Apple (Skin to the Core)*, is in fiction, poetry, memoir, drama, painting, and photography, and he has been widely published and shown.

dellas

Angry Red Planet

Released in 1959, a dozen years before Bowie posed the same
question, this movie trailer asked if there is Life on Mars. You
knew it was *The Angry Red Planet* in question. The Coming Soon
commercial insisted you'd be astounded by "CineMagic." They refused
to define this Special Effect, but they claimed Martian geography would
seem believable. Even at twelve, you'd been fooled frequently enough
to know CineMagic was a lure, snagging gullible fools to enter movie
theaters again after televisions had invaded most American homes,
glowing cyclops sentinels. The invasion a success, people watched
the Test Pattern for hours, studied the Plains Indian head profile,
perched atop a bullseye, providing brightness and contrast, latitude
and longitude points so programs could beam sharp cathode rays,
delivering convenient defined heroes and their requisite villains.
The commercial did offer glimpses of hostile alien settings and life
forms, so you would witness the heroes' bravery. A forty-foot-tall
undulating Bat-Rat-Spider-Scorpion hybrid, Martian vermin, attacked
the crew who were only acting in self-defense, risking life and limb.

> But beyond the commercial, in full film context, we later understood
> the creature was responding to aggressive invaders, who then destroyed
> its eyesight with a sub-zero ray-gun beam blast, freezing its alien retinas.

> Minutes before, they'd landed on this vibrant distant planet overgrown
> in unknown flora. Only the female scientist caught a fleeting glimpse
> of intelligent native life. The men doubted her eyes, then decided the whole
> crew should leave their ship to explore Mars by destroying life forms. They so

loved their weapons, the Communications Expert crew member literally
gave his gun an affectionate name, kissed its barrel, and posed passionately
for photos, cradling his laser rifle in a lover's embrace, recorded for posterity.

CineMagic, turns out, was a simple filter, oversaturating contrast and
brightness, reducing nuance, flooding the frame in red ranges. All Mars
scenes glowed crimson. This polarization was designed to hide the film's
budget, obscure the exotic planet rendered cheaply in shaded drawings.
But instead of the landscape appearing lusher, the Magic merely reduced
humans to malevolent cartoons, chopping and blasting the red planet's
environment, confidently claiming it as their own, history repeating itself.

By the time they fled for earth, only two survived: predictably the romantic,
flirtatious leads. We'd known them at first sight. The female scientist furtively
dabbed perfume on her pulse points while running tests, and the male captain
inexplicably left his space suit gaping wholly unbuttoned, displaying his hairy
virility for her, so we'd know the other members were expendable, killed to
heighten drama. The male scientist, collapsing frail, weakly got them off
the planet and fainted dead against the gravitational pull of Mars,
blood caressing his lips. Beloved or not, the freeze ray failed
the Communications Expert when he most needed its frigid embrace.

The film is told in flashback. Returning to earth, the surviving scientist
willingly dredged memories to save her secret love, the hairy captain,
now comatose, infected with aggressive Martian life. She must recall:
fainting at the sight of the Red Planet's indigene; screaming when a native

plant defended itself after she cut it, and the captain's rescue response, hacking off its offending limbs; finally remembering how she could defeat his infection.

At twelve, you fall under this spell on TV, Saturday Sci-Fi Theatre, believe
at first that it *is* about Mars and the future of space travel. Your brother reads
Custer Died for Your Sins, lying beneath his beloved Red Power posters.
He saved enough to buy the family this Color TV, from his job, after years
of high school teachers asking why he wasted time attending classes anyway.
He believed you deserved a sliver of middle-class American luxury, and
in full, polarized CineMagic red, you hear the refrain of Manifest Destiny.

When the explorers land, they invoke the Santa Maria's ghost and its spectral companion, the label, "New World." The crew jokes of Hard Tack and Hot Coffee, used to technically honor tribal treaties in subsistence terms alone. The land is quiet (too quiet, of course), and before the female scientist does her scream and faint routine, the male captain, in casual conversation, a cocky grin on his face, lets you know exactly what kind of movie you're watching.

He retrieves his pistol and claims an inheritance, telling his ray-gun-kissing sidekick some family lore. His grandfather claimed a sixth sense made his ears twitch if there were Indians around, especially silent, unseen ones, and he caresses his side arm as if it were his short one. The scientist says if native life exists on this new world, it should be where they've landed, so they strap on and step out into the polarized, blazing red world, buzzing with aspirations of conquest and supremac

In your Rez house, distant dreams of running water dampen by pleasures purchased in this Color TV. But you could not deny the truth your brother wanted you to see. Even in the age of rocket-ships and flag-planting on distant planets instead of earthly land masses, indigenous inhabitants were still cast as obstacles, impediments to conquer in the name of advancement, and your brother believed the cost of a TV was worth it. For now you know, finally, that Indians exist beyond the brightness and contrast of TV Test Patterns, and you are the proof indigenous life survives and thrives, growing stronger unseen, on the surface of This Angry Red Planet.

SHERWIN BITSUI

Sherwin Bitsui, Diné (Navajo), is originally from White Cone, Arizona, on the Navajo Reservation. He is the author of *Shapeshift*, *Flood Song*, and *Dissolve*. In addition to teaching at the Institute of American Indian Arts, he is a member of the faculty at Northern Arizona University.

Ungelbah Dávila

From *Dissolve*

Bluing under a dimming North Star,
the Reservation's ghost
paws cartilage *pincered* from a digital cloud.

Its gnawed bones' opaque sigh—
the pallor of bleached wasp eggs,
throbs on tree knobs
      penciled in with burnt ivory smell.

Rising out of the uranium pond—
home picks: *bird flight*
from a cartouche box,
      it then becomes a chain of floating islands.

Slipping into free-fall,
we drip-pattern: *the somewhere parts,*
our shoulders dissolving

                    in somewhere mud.

The arcing sun whistles
across the mask's abalone brow,
its blurring pouts into a forest
chirping from a lake's bite marks
stamped vertically on this map's windowsill.

Kneeling our thoughts on ellipses
evaporating from ollas of fragrant wet clay—
we saddle the drowning's slippery rim.

A hovering smear
trailing desert washes
fenced in with a murder of mirrors
            illumines the eating groaning over us.

Nibbling blades of winter light:
the goat's bleating leased downwind
pastures among foals dripping out
            of hollowed-out dictionaries.

Jeweled with houseflies,
leather rattles, foil-wrapped,
ferment in beaked masks
            on the shores of evaporating lakes.

This plot, now a hotel garden,
its fountain gushing forth—
the slashed wrists of the Colorado.

CEDAR SIGO

Cedar Sigo is a poet and member of the Suquamish Tribe. His books include *Stranger in Town*, *Language Arts*, and *Royals*. He was the Bagley Wright lecturer for 2019 and a book of these lectures, *Guard the Mysteries*, is forthcoming.

Brian Marr

What did you learn here?
(Old Man House, Suquamish)

How to fall asleep easily on the beach,

    to dig clams, to dream a net made of nettles.

        A medicine of marsh tea boiled out to the open air,

a memory of cedar bark coiled,

resting for months in cold water
        to be fashioned into our so-called lifestyle,

clothes for ceremony
    as well as daily life,
  canoe bailers,
    diapers,
      we used the wood for our half-mile longhouse and totems,
        dried fish, a hard smoke
wooden oval plates that hooked together
filled with clear oil of salmon,

    to wet our palates and smooth our bodies.

    A shawl of woolly dog (now extinct)
      they were bred on tiny islands
  we can still identify,

Tatoosh Island off of Cape Flattery where there were whaling tribes too,

the Makah,
                    one of whose villages collapsed,
preserved in silt (later unearthed) and how else?

          Which other ceremonies or necessary edges of objects?

          Our ivory needles, otter pelts, mat creasers, our dances.

What else do you remember dreaming of?

A kind of rake to skim the waves, to catch tiny fish on rows of twisted nails.

LAURA TOHE

Laura Tohe, Diné (Navajo), is Sleepy Rock People clan and born for the Bitter Water People. An award-winning poet and recipient of the 2020 Academy of American Poets Laureate Fellowship, she has written four books, including *Code Talker Stories*; a chapbook; and two librettos for oratorios that were performed in Phoenix, Arizona, and in Rouen and Caen, France.

J. Morgan Edwards

Within Dinétah the People's Spirit Remains Strong

These words are for my people, the Diné, who endured colossal hardship and near death and continue to endure

In the people's memory are the stories
This we remember:

I

Ałkidąą' adajiní nt'ę́ę́'.
They say long time ago in time immemorial:
the stories say we emerged from
the umbilical center of this sacred earth into the Glittering World
smoothed by Twin Heroes,
sons of White Shell Woman,
who journeyed to find their father
and aided by Spider Woman who taught them
how not to fear the perilous journey.
They say the sun, father to the Twin Heroes,
gave them the knowledge to slay the monsters
so that the world would be safe.

We lived according to the teachings of the Holy People
to dwell within the sacred mountains:
Sisnaajiní rising to the east,
Tsoodził rising to the south,
Dook'o'osłííd rising to the west,

Dibé Nítsaa rising to the north.
We raised our families,
planted our corn,
greeted the dawn with our prayers,
and followed the path of corn pollen.
Every day was a new beginning
 . . . in Beauty
 . . . in Beauty.

II

The ancestors predicted it would happen,
that the wind would shift and bring
light-colored men from across the big water
who would shatter our world.
They would arrive wearing metal coats
riding strange beautiful animals,
would arrive in clothes that brushed the earth
carrying crossed sticks to plunge into Dinétah.
In their zealous urge they sought cities of gold.
Later we learned they came to take
our land, our lives, our spirits.

Did they not know we are
all created from the same elements?
Rainclouds for hair,
fingernails formed from beautiful seashells,
the rivers flow through our veins, our lifeline,
from wind we came to life,
with thunder voices we speak.
We fought back to protect ourselves
as we had fought with other enemies.

The world changed when
the light-colored men brought their women.
It was then we knew they meant to stay.
They invented ways to justify what they wanted,
Manifest Destiny, assimilation, colonization.
And, most of all, they wanted the land.
One day a man wearing red clothes appeared.
"Bi'éé' "Łichii'í, Kit Carson, sent by Wáashindoon.
He brought many soldiers.
They spoke with thunder sticks
that tore into everything that we loved,
to burn our beautiful peach orchards,
to slaughter our sheep in front of us,
to starve us out from Dinétah,
to do unspeakable things to us,
to wrench us from our land.
What strange fruit is this that dangles

from the trees?
We feared for our lives
and hid among the rocks and shadows
gathering food and water when we could.

III

What was our crime?
We wanted only to live as we had
within our sacred mountains
seeking harmony, seeking long life
... in Beauty
... in Beauty.

Others had their death march:
The Trail of Tears, Auschwitz,
The Door of No Return in the House of Slaves.
We are Diné.
We too had our death march forced on us.
When The Long Walk began we witnessed our women murdered and raped
our children and relatives swept away in the rushing currents
        of the Rio Grande river.
We heard explosions that silenced mothers giving birth behind the rocks.
We saw the newborn and the elderly left behind.
We saw our warriors unable to defend us.

And even now the land we crossed still holds
	the memory of our people's tears, cries, and blood.
Kit Carson marched us three hundred miles away.
In the distance we saw our sacred mountains
	becoming smaller and smaller.
We were torn from the land that held our birth stems.
We were taken to the land that was not us.
We were taken to the desolate place without trees or vegetation
where the men picked out undigested corn from animal dung to eat,
where young women were raped.
We called this place Hwééldi,
this place of starvation,
this place of near death,
this place of extreme hardship.

IV

We returned to our land after four years.
Our spirits ragged and weary.
And vowed that we never be separated from Dinétah;
	the earth is our strength.
We have grown strong.
We are the children of White Shell Woman.
We are the people of the original clans she created.
We are female warriors and male warriors—Manuelito, Barboncito
We are the Code Talkers who used our language to help save America.

We are Annie Wauneka who taught us to have faith in the white man's medicine.
We are the sons and daughters of activists and other unsung heroes
      "when Indian men were the finest men there were."
We are the hands that create fine turquoise and silver jewelry.
We are the women who resisted relocation when the government came with papers
      and fences.
We are teachers, cowboys, lawyers, musicians.
We are medicine people, doctors, nurses, college professors.
We are artists, soldiers, politicians, architects, farmers.
We are sheep herders, engineers, singers, comediennes.
We are weavers of baskets and exquisite blankets.
We are bus drivers, welders, ranchers, dishwashers.
We are the people who offer prayers during the cycles of the day.
We are Diné.
In Beauty it was begun.
In Beauty it continues.
    In Beauty,

      In Beauty,

        In Beauty,

          In Beauty.

LAYLI LONG SOLDIER

Layli Long Soldier is the author of *Whereas*. She is a citizen of the Oglala Lakota Nation and currently resides in Santa Fe, New Mexico.

Nancy Nichols

Resolution 2

I

commend   this land

and   this   land

honor   this   land

Native   ☐   this   land

Peoples   this land

for   this   land

the   this   land

thousands   this   land

of   this   land

years   this   land

that   this land

they   this   land have   this   land

stewarded   this   land

and   this   land

protected   this land   this land   this land   this land   this land   this land   this

this

LUCI TAPAHONSO

Luci Tapahonso is Diné (Navajo) and grew up in Shiprock, New Mexico. She served as the inaugural Navajo Nation poet laureate (2013–15) and is emerita professor of English literature and languages at the University of New Mexico.

CJ Heatley III

Ilíígo[2] Naalyéhé:[3] Goods of Value

Yes, those days are over;
our childhoods were immersed in ílíígo hané[4]—
Diné stories and songs that were conveyed with delight, reverence,
or sometimes tears. Hané is always bound with comfort.
When the grown-ups began talking, we paused our loud play and tussling
and squeezed in at the table or settled on the floor nearby.
Our visceral need and appreciation for stories took over
as we absorbed the rhythm, pauses, rises and falls in their voices.
Something inside us urged us to remember, not to forget.
We also knew the exact tone, that slight dip in tenor when we had to leave
    the room.
It is said that a child's ears and mind are vulnerable.
They would say, "Nihi 'áłchíni niłhil a'yóo da'íłí—
we hold our children in much respect."

Decades later, we share the same stories with our children and grandchildren
this time mixed with English. We sing the same songs.
Our children have learned to listen and to ascertain
whether they could ask questions. In time they, too, grasped the intent,

1 Ilíígo: An item or idea that is literally and/or figuratively of great value. It is also used
to describe a person who is well respected, someone who is dignified.

3 Naalyéhé: An item that one carries about which has significant cultural import; some-
thing that is cherished and has heft.

3 Hané: Stories that are told and retold over generations.

the underlying resolve in the pauses, smiles, dips and echoes of saad[5]—
the wisdom of the old words, long prayers, and timeless songs.

The adults who surrounded us in childhood are gone now—iná kaí.
They have left on their journey, but their hané and songs remain.
The prayers, laughter, and songs that guided them into sá[6]
—old age—
remain with us.

Áa bił dáhwiłiłį 'ńtęé. It was their saad—verbal properties—
a form of soft goods[7] that kept them steady.
Saad strengthens our minds and bodies
like a sis łigáaí,[8] the silver belt that encircles
one's waist to keep our posture upright.
They used to say, "The Holy Ones will see us coming
at a distance, adorned with stories and jewelry,
and they will murmur, "'Ashi néé, shi awee, my beloved little ones.'"
Thus, we honor them by wearing the jewelry they created

---

4 Saad: Songs, prayers, and stories that comprise traditional knowledge and wisdom.

6 Sá: Old age; an elder who has acquired valuable knowledge throughout his or her long life.

7 Soft goods: Refers to items that are pliable such as fabric and blankets as well as intangible gifts such as stories, words of encouragement, and teachings. Hard goods refer to material items such as jewelry, firewood, and tools.

8 Sis łigáaí: A handmade belt made of silver (łigáaí means white) and turquoise stones; commonly known as a concha belt.

and we revere the world they put into place for us:
the mountains, rivers, sky, plants, stars, birds and animals.
'Éí 'ałdó' ílíígo naalyéhé at'e—they, too, have great value.

Like our elders, our hope is that the young ones become diné[9] bił da'ílíngi—
persons of virtue—a man who helps when a stranger's car stalls,
the one who offers the exact words of comfort when needed,
gives a soft hug or holds your hand in silence.
The one who cooks for the grief-stricken
when the hours become a blur and exhaustion hovers at the doorways
and the scents of stew, just-baked bread and coffee linger.
Or the person turns an ordinary day into a jovial gathering
complete with ílíígo hané and chi'yáán łikaní[10]—
good stories and tasty dishes. The house again fills with
outbursts of delight when relatives arrive.

We trust that the young ones will offer a bed to relatives
who would otherwise sleep curled against cement buildings
or panhandle on street corners—distraught and thin—
beset by chemical cravings our ancestors could not fathom.
They are kin who have veered from their íłįígo hané;
For them, the stories are echoes that can't be named
like the resonating childhood voices that visit on the coldest nights.

9 Diné: A Navajo man (singular) or the Navajo people.
10 Chi'yáán łikaní: Tasty dishes; memorable meals.

They pawned the family's hard goods, the íłįígo naalyéhé,
the valuables that were carried about as hané,
the saad at the spiral center of the taut basket
that was created to weave the past into our present and future.

Still, we are grateful for the women who still wear long skirts
and turquoise jewelry as if each day is sacred,
They say, "Shí íłįígo naalyéhé bił naasó naashá do—
I will go forth into the day clothed in my shields."
They were bestowed with hard goods
at their first laugh dinner. Their parents, too,
always wore a bracelet, earrings or a bolo tie.

They remember the times of crisis when
everyone held each other and prayed
while clasping soft pouches of corn pollen.

Now they carry their childhood offerings
throughout the day as overhead,
the sun's many-colored horses gallop across the sky.

NATALIE DIAZ

Natalie Diaz, author most recently of *Postcolonial Love Poem*, was born and raised in the Fort Mojave Indian Village. She is Mojave, Akimel O'otham, and an enrolled member of the Gila River Indian Community.

Arizona State University

Postcolonial Love Poem

I've been taught bloodstones can cure a snakebite,
can stop the bleeding—most people forgot this
when the war ended. The war ended
depending on which war you mean: those we started,
before those, millennia ago and onward,
those which started me, which I lost and won—
these ever-blooming wounds.
I was built by wage. So I wage Love and worse—
always another campaign to march across
a desert night for the cannon flash of your pale skin
settling in a silver lagoon of smoke at your breast.
I dismount my dark horse, bend to you there, deliver you
the hard pull of all my thirsts—
I learned *Drink* in a country of drought.
We pleasure to hurt, leave marks
the size of stones—each a cabochon polished
by our mouths. I, your lapidary, your lapidary wheel
turning—green mottled red—
the jaspers of our desires.
There are wildflowers in my desert
which take up to twenty years to bloom.
The seeds sleep like geodes beneath hot feldspar sand
until a flash flood bolts the arroyo, lifting them
in its copper current, opens them with memory—
they remember what their god whispered
into their ribs: *Wake up and ache for your life.*
Where your hands have been are diamonds

on my shoulders, down my back, thighs—
I am your culebra.
I am in the dirt for you.
Your hips are quartz-light and dangerous,
two rose-horned rams ascending a soft desert wash
before the November sky unyokes a hundred-year flood—
the desert returned suddenly to its ancient sea.
Arise the wild heliotrope, scorpion weed,
blue phacelia which hold purple the way a throat can hold
the shape of any great hand—
Great hands is what she called mine.
The rain will eventually come, or not.
Until then, we touch our bodies like wounds—
The war never ended and somehow begins again.

Acknowledgments

I express gratitude for the opportunity to share these poems. This project includes forty-seven contemporary Native Nations poets, a sampling from many who write poetry in these times. I remain thankful for their inspiration and for their teachers, including their poetry ancestors, which include American and world poets back to the beginning. I especially wish to acknowledge the Kiowa poet N. Scott Momaday, who remains a respected elder of contemporary Native Nations poetry and has inspired and influenced all of us.

There would be no anthology without the *Living Nations, Living Words* project, and there would be no such project without the staff of the Library of Congress. I have worked closely with Literary Initiatives staff; they are insightful, creative, inspirational, and they assisted in every detail to bring this vision forward. The Geography and Map Division staff worked diligently to help us realize the web map from which the poets emerge. The American Folklife Center staff assembled the poems, recordings, transcripts, and photographs into a permanent collection of Native Nations poets. The Publishing Office staff helped see the project through with their meticulous feedback and direction on the anthology. Literary Director Marie Arana believed in and supported the vision of the project and the book. At the helm is the inspirational Librarian of Congress, Dr. Carla Hayden. This collection is evidence of her management, her hard work, and her goodwill. I must add a special acknowledgement of Rob Casper and Anne Holmes, who saw to the care of this project from the beginning.

My editor at W. W. Norton, Jill Bialosky, has been with me through most of my literary path. I am most grateful to her belief and her direction. I also wish to acknowledge her assistant, Drew Elizabeth Weitman, who has seen us through this anthology and has shepherded me through many other projects. I am grateful for my assistant, Jennifer Elise Foerster, who is the best partner in literary accomplishment anyone could have by their side.

And always, gratitude for this earth and the gifts of this earth, including trees for paper, the materials for ink, which leads us to the sun and the rain and the singers of plants. And to all those who have seen and will see this publication from the roots of an idea to the completion of a map, to this anthology, which includes the copyeditors, printers, bookmakers, drivers, and others who get this collection into your hands and your ears.

Mvto, which is "thank you" in the Mvskoke language.

Credits

b: william bearhart, "Transplant: After Georgia O'Keeffe's *Pelvis IV, 1944*" first published in *Tinderbox Poetry Journal*, volume 2, issue 4 (December 2015). Copyright © by b: william bearhart. Reprinted with the permission of the author. Photo by Thomas Lindfors, courtesy of the author.

Sherwin Bitsui, ["Bluing under a dimming North Star,"] from *Dissolve*. Copyright © 2018 by Sherwin Bitsui. Reprinted with the permission of The Permissions Company, LLC on behalf of Copper Canyon Press, www.coppercanyonpress.org. Photo courtesy of photographer Ungelbah Dávila.

Kimberly Blaeser, "Poem on Disappearance." Copyright © by Kimberly Blaeser. Photo by John Fisher, courtesy of the author.

Heather Cahoon, "Baby Out of Cut-Open Woman" from *Horsefly Dress* by Heather Cahoon. Copyright © 2020 by Heather Cahoon. Reprinted by permission of the University of Arizona Press. Photo courtesy of the author.

Laura Da', "The Rhetorical Feminine" first published in *The Rumpus* (April 2020). Copyright © by Laura Da'. Reprinted with the permission of the author. Photo by Jarrod Da', courtesy of the author.

Natalie Diaz, "Postcolonial Love Poem" from *Postcolonial Love Poem*. Copyright © 2020 by Natalie Diaz. Reprinted with the permission of The Permissions Company, LLC on behalf of Graywolf Press, Minneapolis, Minnesota, graywolfpress.org. Photo by Arizona State University, courtesy of the author.

Anita Endrezze, "Thirteen Ways of Looking at an Indian" from *Enigma* (Press 53, 2019). Copyright © by Anita Endrezze. Reprinted with the permission of the author. Photo by Maja Hansen, courtesy of the author.

Luci Tapahonso, "Ilíígo Naalyéhé: Goods of Value." Copyright © by Luci Tapahonso. Photo by C. J. Heatley III, courtesy of the author.

Laura Tohe, "Within Dinétah the People's Spirit Remains Strong" first published in *Explorations in Navajo Poetry and Poetics*, edited by Anthony K. Webster (University of New Mexico Press, 2009). Copyright © by Laura Tohe. Reprinted with the permission of the author. Photo by J. Morgan Edwards, courtesy of the author.

Tanaya Winder, "like any good indian woman" first published in *World Literature Today* (May 2017). Copyright © by Tanaya Winder. Reprinted with the permission of the author. Photo by Viki Eagle, courtesy of the author.

Elizabeth Woody, "Coquille." Copyright © by Elizabeth Woody. Photo by Native Arts and Cultures Foundation (NACF), courtesy of the author.

Ray Young Bear, "*Wichihaka*/The One I Live With" from *Manifestation Wolverine: The Collected Poetry of Ray Young Bear* (Open Road Media, 2015). Copyright © by Ray Young Bear. Reprinted with the permission of the author. Photo by Stella Lasley-Young Bear, courtesy of the author.

Ofelia Zepeda, "B 'o E-a:g maṣ 'ab Him g Ju:kǐ/It is Going to Rain" from the bilingual audio CD chapbook *Jeweḍ 'I-hoi/Earth Movements* (Kore Press, 1997). Copyright © by Ofelia Zepeda. Reprinted with the permission of Kore Press. korepress.org. Photo by Tony Celentano, courtesy of the author.

Index